HEINEMANN HISTORY

STUDY UNITS

IMPERIAL CHINA

Fiona Reynoldson

Heinemann Library,
an imprint of Heinemann Publishers (Oxford) Ltd,
Halley Court, Jordan Hill, Oxford OX2 8EJ

OXFORD LONDON EDINBURGH MADRID
ATHENS BOLOGNA PARIS MELBOURNE
SYDNEY AUCKLAND SINGAPORE TOKYO
IBADAN NAIROBI HARARE GABORONE
PORTSMOUTH NH (USA)

This edition first published 1994

98 97 96 95 94

10 9 8 7 6 5 4 3 2 1

**British Library Cataloguing in Publication Data is available
from the British Library on request.**

ISBN 0–431–07351–1

Designed by Ron Kamen, Green Door Design Ltd, Basingstoke

Illustrated by Jane Cheswright and Jeff Edwards

Printed in China

The front cover shows part of the Terracotta Army guarding
the tomb of the First Emperor.

The back cover shows a soldier from the Terracotta Army.

Acknowledgements

The author and publisher would like to thank the following
for permission to reproduce photographs:

Ancient Art & Architecture Collection: 4.4A, 5.7A
Archiv für Kunst und Geschichte, Berlin: 2.6B
Aspect Picture Library: 4.1C
Trustees of the British Museum: 3.1A, 4.3B
China Photo Library Ltd: Front and back cover
C. M. Dixon: 2.4D
Edinburgh University Library: 5.8A
Werner Forman Archive/British Library: 1.3A
Werner Forman Archive/Eskenau Ltd, London: 2.2C, 5.4A
Werner Forman Archive/Idemitsu Museum of Arts, Tokyo:
4.2A
Robert Harding Picture Library: 2.7C, 3.1B, 3.4C, 5.1A
Michael Holford: 5.3C
MacQuitty International Collection: 3.2A
Museum of Fine Arts, Boston: 5.2A
Trustees of the Science Museum: 5.7B
Xinhua News Agency: 1.1A, 1.1B, 1.2A, 1.3B, 2.2A, 2.3A,
2.3B, 2.4A, 2.5A, 2.5B, 2.5E, 2.5F, 2.6A, 3.3A, 3.5A, 3.5D,
4.1A, 5.1B, 5.3A, 5.3B, 5.8C

Every effort has been made to contact copyright holders of
material reproduced in this book. Any omissions will be
rectified in subsequent printings if notice is given to the
publisher.

Details of written sources

In some sources the wording or sentence structure has been
simplified to ensure that the source is accessible.

J. Bronowski, *The Ascent of Man*, BBC, 1973: 5.8B
Arthur Cotterell, *The First Emperor of China*, Macmillan,
1981: 2.4B, 2.5C, 2.5D, 2.7A, 2.7B
Bamber Gascoigne, *Treasures and Dynasties of China*, Jonathon
Cape, 1973: 2.4C, 4.3A, 4.4C
R. W. L. Guisso, C. Pagani, D. Miller, *The First Emperor of
China*, Sidgwick and Jackson, 1989: 2.1A, 2.1B, 2.1C, 2.2B
Mencius from R. W. L. Guisso, C. Pagani, D. Miller, *The First
Emperor of China*, Sidgwick and Jackson, 1989: 5.5A
Joseph Needham, 'Science and China's influence on the
West', from Raymond Dawson, *The Legacy of China*, OUP,
1964: 3.5C, 4.1B
J. H. San, *Ancient China's Inventions*, The Commercial Press,
Hong Kong, 1984: 2.3B, 3.5B, 5.6A
R. Whitfield, A. Farrer, *The Caves of a Thousand Buddhas*,
British Museum, 1990: 5.2B
Bai Xingjian, 'Story of a singsong girl', from *Collection of
Stories from the Tang Dynasty*, Foreign Language Press, 1954:
5.4B

We have tried to use Pinyin spellings throughout this book.
However, to avoid confusion, old spellings for more familiar
Chinese names and places have been retained.

CONTENTS

1.1 Finding out about Ancient China

China is surrounded by mountains, deserts and the sea. In its early history it was isolated from the rest of the world. This isolation helped it to develop an independent civilization. It was not the earliest civilization in the world, but no other civilization has had such a long and continuous history.

We divide history into particular periods. In Britain, periods of history are often called after the name of the king or queen who reigned at the time. For instance, the Victorian period is when Queen Victoria reigned (1837–1901). In China, periods of history are called after dynasties. A **dynasty** is the period of time during which a royal family was ruling under an emperor. For example, the Qin dynasty was when the King of Qin became emperor and his son ruled after him.

We know about ancient China from three main sources:

Archaeology: finding objects from the past buried in the ground. A tomb at Mawangdui from the time of the Han dynasty (see timeline) contains everything a rich woman needed in her afterlife. Archaeologists found silk clothes, shoes, mirrors, coins, medicines and 152 small wooden tomb figures dressed in silk, representing servants. There were also bowls and food.

Written sources: anything written down – stories, prayers, history books, household accounts, census returns, military orders, recipes for gunpowder etc. There are inscriptions scratched on to bones that date from about 1400 BC. There are names on bronze containers dating from the Shang dynasty.

Tombs give Chinese archaeologists much of the evidence about the past. These jade clothes covered the dead body of Queen Dou Wan of the Han dynasty. The Chinese believed that jade preserved life. However, when this tomb was opened, the body inside the jade suit had crumbled to dust. The upper parts of the jade suit were lying flat on top of the lower parts.

A

SOURCE

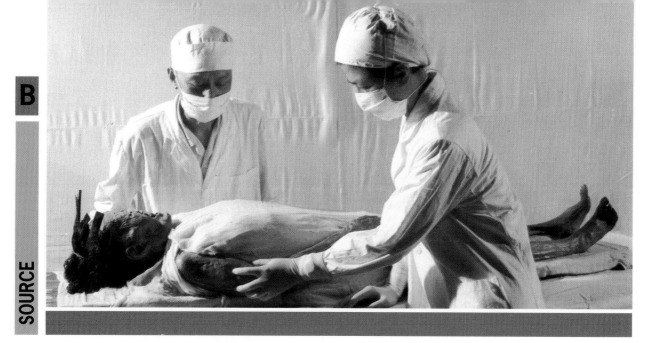

There are written orders to soldiers serving on the Great Wall. By the time of the Han dynasty there were already 9,000 characters in the Chinese language referring to food. The first surviving cookbook giving quantities of ingredients dates from the 10th century AD. It is by Madame Wu of Jiangsu. We also have official histories of the reigns of many of the emperors.

This is the body of a woman of about 50 years of age. She was embalmed and buried about 2,000 years ago. She was not covered with jade.

Artefacts: things people have made that are still there for us to see – the Great Wall of China, paintings, buildings etc.

This timeline covers Chinese history between 500 BC and AD 1400.

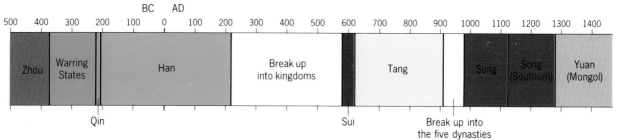

Wang Mang

We know about Wang Mang (died AD 23) because a history of his reign was written after he died. He was a nephew of an empress of the Han dynasty. He was clever and powerful. When a new emperor was chosen, Wang Mang became regent. Then he decided to become emperor himself, thus bringing to an end the first part of the Han dynasty in AD 9.

Wang Mang was a very busy emperor. He took land from the rich and gave it to farmers. He did away with slavery. He helped farmers by setting up huge warehouses to store grain. The farmers could buy it cheaply from him when there was a shortage. Wang Mang also reformed the money system but his new idea was so complicated that no one could understand it. He called in all the gold in China and gave bronze in return. This meant that he had a huge amount of gold but had annoyed many people. Wang Mang was overthrown in AD 23 and the Han dynasty was restored.

1.2 How do we Know?

The richest source that we have for finding out about ancient China is archaeology. China has many archaeological sites for two main reasons.

One reason is that the land of China has been lived in for many thousands of years. In particular, people have been farming and living in one place for about 10,000 years. They buried their dead in and near their villages and archaeologists have been able to excavate the tombs.

Archaeologists uncovering horses and chariots from a tomb 2,200 years old.

The second reason why we know so much is that the Chinese believed in an **afterlife**. As the population of China grew, people living in villages banded together into tribes. Some people were leaders and were considered more important than others. They had larger tombs in which were placed all the things the dead person might need in the afterlife. These give us valuable clues to their way of life and beliefs. In early times, servants, soldiers and animals were often killed and placed in tombs. They were meant to look after the people in the next world. There were also bowls of food, clothes and weapons.

Linked to the belief in the afterlife was the Chinese reverence for their **ancestors**. This is often called ancestor worship. It was very important that dead people were properly buried and were remembered. This reverence for ancestors extended into life too. The Chinese revered the elderly. In every day life, people looked up to and obeyed their elder relatives.

A

SOURCE

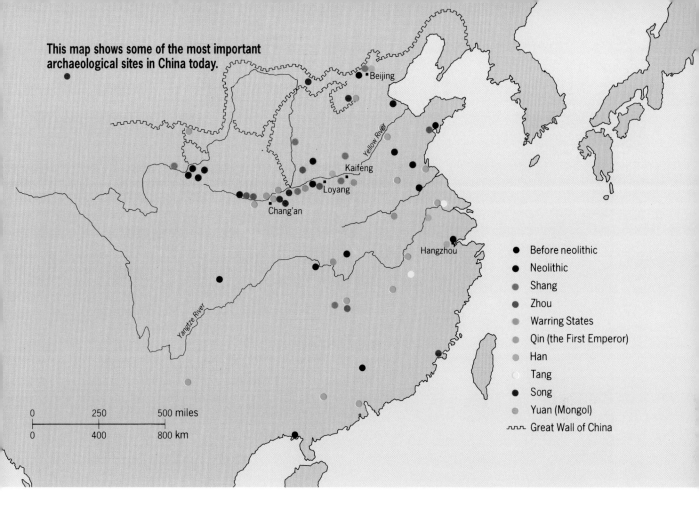

This map shows some of the most important archaeological sites in China today.

Beijing

Yellow River

Kaifeng

Loyang

Chang'an

Hangzhou

Yangtze River

● Before neolithic
● Neolithic
● Shang
● Zhou
● Warring States
● Qin (the First Emperor)
● Han
○ Tang
● Song
● Yuan (Mongol)
ᴖᴖ Great Wall of China

| 0 | 250 | 500 miles |
| 0 | 400 | 800 km |

They in turn looked up to the government. The emperor was at the very top of this social structure – like a tiled roof on a brick house.

This stability in society continued despite wars and invasions. The other strand of continuity in Chinese history has been **agriculture**. The vast majority of Chinese people were farmers. Emperors came and went but the farmers went on growing food year after year and century after century.

The idea of an emperor who ruled over the whole of China went back into the mists of legend. However, we have firm evidence of emperors from the time of the First Emperor in 221 BC. From that time until AD 1911 there were 210 emperors and one empress. In 1911 there was a revolution. A new form of government was set up.

Peking Man

There was great excitement in the 1920s. A skeleton of a man dating from about half a million years ago was found near Peking in China. This was the oldest skeleton of a human being found so far.

Finding the skeleton gave archaeology in China a big start. Since that time many digs have been carried out and some wonderful finds have been made.

However, Peking Man himself was no sooner found than he was lost again. The skeleton remains were put in crates. But then the Japanese invaded China. The crates were taken from one place to another as the Japanese army advanced deep into China. Somehow, in all the chaos, they were lost.

1.3 Chinese Writing

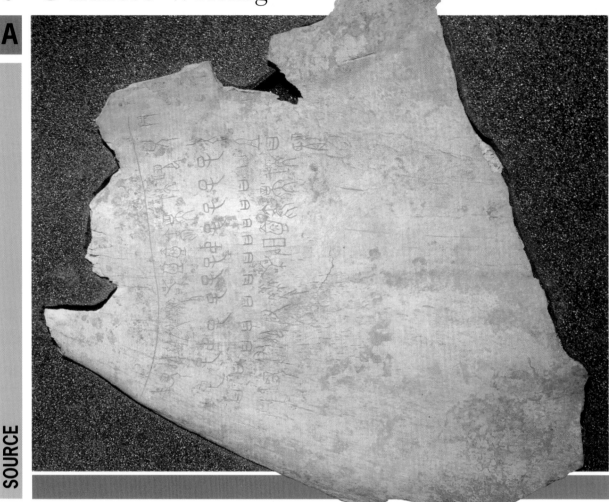

Chinese writing was well developed by 1400 BC. The earliest writing we know of is on **oracle bones**. These bones were usually the shoulder bones of large animals such as sheep or oxen, but tortoiseshells were also used. The bones were used for **divination** (foretelling the future). Ancient Chinese people wanted to know what was going to happen. They would ask about anything in the future. Was it safe to go on a journey? Was it a good time to fight a war? The questions were written on the bone and then it was heated. People believed that the cracks in the bone would tell them what was going to happen. Nearly 100,000 of these bones and tortoiseshells have been found since 1900.

Writing has also been found on bronze objects from about 1300 BC. Often the writing includes the name of the maker and shows that the object was made for a particular person.

An oracle bone from about 1400 BC. Thousands of these bones were found during excavations at Anyang (the Shang dynasty capital). The names of Shang kings were written on many of them. When these bones were discovered, this was the first firm evidence that some of these legendary figures had in fact existed.

A bronze axe head from the Shang dynasty (about 1500-1100 BC). It was discovered in 1966. Many Shang bronzes have inscriptions on them.

In our alphabet, each letter stands for one sound. We put sounds together to build up a word. In Chinese writing, each **character** or 'picture' is a word in itself. This works well for things. The picture of a horse means a horse. Even a horse running is not difficult to draw. It is far more difficult to make pictures meaning 'liking' or 'shadow' or 'to go up'. To solve this, the Chinese made up an enormous number of characters. They put two or more characters together to make different meanings understood. They even made some of their characters stand for sounds.

Characters used between 1400 and 1200 BC and still in use today. They mean 'shadow', 'up to' and 'horse'.

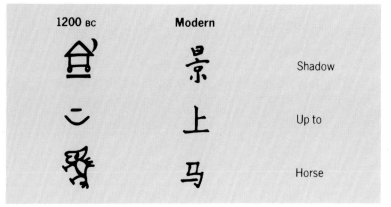

1200 BC	Modern	
		Shadow
		Up to
		Horse

Wade

Sir Thomas Wade (1818–95) was a British soldier who was very good at languages. He was sent out to China at the time of the Opium Wars (1839–42) and learnt Chinese on the ship while he was travelling.

Translating the Chinese character writing into alphabet writing was called romanization. Wade worked out a very good system of romanization. Another man called Herbert Giles improved Wade's method. Thus the standard romanization for many years was called the Wade-Giles system.

2.1 The Warring States

In the time of the **Warring States**, before the First Emperor, the many states of China fought among themselves nearly all the time. The state of Qin fought fifteen major wars between 364 BC and 234 BC. When the states were not fighting they were bargaining with each other.

Two or three states would make an **alliance** and agree to join together to fight another state. Then one of the states would betray another and change sides. Every state used bribes to buy **allies** (friends). Sometimes these bribes were money or silk. Sometimes they were people. Princesses were sent as wives to rulers of other states. Dancing girls were sent as gifts. At other times, instead of a bribe, hostages were exchanged. Of course if the alliance between the states broke up the hostages were killed.

A **SOURCE** Li Si was a clerk in the state of Chu. One day he entered his office privy (lavatory). He noticed that the rats were scrawny and filthy. In the granary near the office the rats were fat and arrogant. 'A man's life is just like that of the rats,' he thought. 'His condition depends on where he places himself.' Li Si realized that Qin was fast becoming the strongest of the seven states. He travelled there in 247 BC.

From the 'Shiji', written in about 100 BC. This extract is based on the writings of Li Si who became the First Emperor's chief minister. He was writing in about 210 BC.

The main states conquered by Qin to form China under the First Emperor.

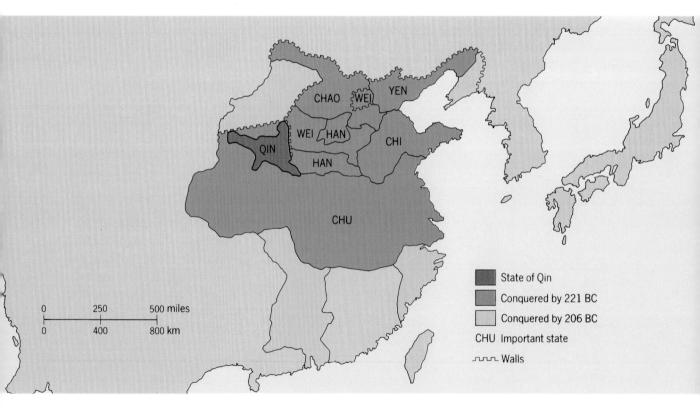

0 250 500 miles
0 400 800 km

■ State of Qin
■ Conquered by 221 BC
■ Conquered by 206 BC
CHU Important state
ᴖᴖᴖᴖ Walls

B

SOURCE

Qin's frontier defences are mountains. It has forests, streams and valleys. Entering its frontiers, I saw that the people were simple and plain. Their music was simple. Their clothing was plain and not frivolous. They stood in deep awe of the officials and followed the old customs obediently. When I entered the cities, I saw that the officials were dignified, courteous, honest and sincere. They are worthy men.

From the 'Shiji', based on the writings of Xun Zi who was writing in about 240 BC.

C

SOURCE

For four generations now, Qin has won easy victory. Its armies are the strongest in the world. It did not reach this position by goodness or worthiness, but by taking advantage of every opportunity. That is all.

From the 'Shiji', based on the writings of Li Si who was writing in about 210 BC.

It was all very well for a king of a state to win battles and gain land, but if he could not rule well he lost it all again. Many clever men made careers advising the different kings. They travelled from state to state selling their advice. This custom went back to the 5th century BC. That was when **Confucius** lived (see also page 28). Confucius is the most famous Chinese scholar and thinker. He was one of these advisers and told kings how to rule, make laws and how to tax the ordinary people.

Most of what we know about the First Emperor of China comes from archaeological sources and from China's first important history book that has survived. This book is called the **'Shiji'**. It was written by Sima Qian. He wrote it 100 years after the time of the First Emperor and he did not approve of him. So we have to be careful when using the book.

According to the *Shiji*, the First Emperor was born in 259 BC. He was the illegitimate son of a merchant and the King of Qin's **concubine** (one of many wives). No one knew his real father was a merchant, so in time he became King of Qin.

By the time the First Emperor was born the 200 or so small states were joined into seven, large, powerful kingdoms. Qin was the most powerful of these. The Warring States period ended when the King of Qin defeated all the other states. That was when he declared himself the First Emperor of China, in 221 BC.

Sima Qian

Sima Qian (145–85 BC) inherited his father's post of Grand Historian at the court of the Han. For centuries, his family had been historians and officials at court. He is famous for writing the *Shiji*, the first history of China from mythological times up to the early years of the Han dynasty. It covers events, lives of great people and treatises. These treatises are about things like building canals, non-Chinese people, the calendar, and more.

Sima Qian was castrated for trying to defend a general who had surrendered to the northern tribes. He was disgraced, but he was determined to finish the *Shiji* to honour his father. The book is the first attempt to write a history of the world as the Chinese knew it.

2.2 The First Emperor

By 221 BC, the King of Qin had defeated the other six kingdoms. He declared himself the **First Emperor of China** and determined to bring the wars to an end once and for all to unite China. The ordinary people of China must have welcomed this. Most of them were peasants who lived by farming. The constant wars meant they had to leave their farms to go and fight. Their crops of wheat and rice were stolen, they paid higher taxes and many were killed. Life under the new Emperor had to be better. In some ways it was.

Li Si, the Emperor's favourite adviser, told the Emperor not to hand out land to his sons and army leaders. Far better for the Emperor to keep control of all the empire himself. The Emperor agreed. He gave money and presents to his sons and army leaders instead. He told them that he had brought peace and from now on he would rule alone.

He divided China into 36 areas. In turn he divided the areas into smaller districts. There were three departments in each area:

1 **The military department** was headed by a military governor or official. This dealt with everything to do with the army – from recruiting soldiers to paying and clothing them.

2 **The civil department** was under a civil governor or official. It dealt with everything concerning the ordinary people: from taxpaying to keeping the law.

3 **The inspection department** was headed by the imperial inspector or official. This official reported direct to the Emperor. This is how the Emperor kept up to date with what was happening all over China. It also made sure that what was happening was approved by the Emperor. By knowing what was going on, he could stop the military and civil officials from becoming too powerful.

A

SOURCE

A portrait of the First Emperor, probably painted in the 17th century AD.

The officials were all paid by the Emperor and could be sacked by him. They could not pass on their jobs to their sons. The men chosen for the jobs were well educated and loyal. This is the beginning of China becoming a centralized state. All the decisions and power rested with the Emperor in his capital, in the centre of China.

The First Emperor has the proboscis (nose) of a hornet and large all-seeing eyes. His chest is like that of a bird of prey and his voice like that of a jackal. He is merciless; with the heart of a tiger or wolf. When he is in trouble, he finds it easy to humble himself (and ask advice) but when he is enjoying success, he finds it just as easy to devour human beings.

From the 'Shiji', based on the writings of Wei Liao, a favourite adviser of the King of Qin, before he became First Emperor.

Reverse side of a bronze mirror. The other side is highly polished. Mirrors were very popular. There are many legends about how suspicious the First Emperor was. One says that he had a mirror about 2 metres across that could reveal the internal organs of anyone who stood before it. It would also show up their innermost thoughts.

Chu Yuan

Chu Yuan (died 288 BC) was a poet who lived in the kingdom of Chu in the Warring States period. (Chu is shown on the map on page 10.) Chu Yuan was related to the King of Chu and would have liked to have had an official position in the government. However, since he criticized the king's policy towards the kingdom or state of Qin, he did not get the job he wanted. Chu Yuan was very disappointed. He could see that the ruler of Qin was determined to conquer as much land as he could and would stop at nothing to get what he wanted. Chu Yuan was quite right. The state of Qin steadily conquered all the other states around. By 221 BC, the King of Qin had defeated all the other kingdoms and made himself the First Emperor.

Chu Yuan devoted himself to writing poetry. He was the first Chinese person to become famous as a poet. His longest poem is called 'On Encountering Sorrow' and is part of a collection of his poems called *Songs of the South*. For hundreds of years his poems were part of the curriculum for study in China. Chu did not live to see his country conquered. He is said to have committed suicide by jumping into a river. His death is commemorated to this day by the Dragon Boat Festival which takes place every year in China.

2.3 Running the Empire

The First Emperor needed clever men to advise him. He chose Li Si, a **Legalist** as his favourite adviser. Legalists believed that all people were basically bad. They would only obey the law if they were afraid of being punished. Therefore, punishments for breaking the law must be very harsh. Under the First Emperor they were. Beheading, cutting in half or being torn apart by chariots were normal capital punishments. Cutting off the nose, ears, genitals and feet were other punishments. Probably the most usual punishment, however, was forced labour.

Thousands and thousands of **convicts** (prisoners), dressed in red, often tatooed or with their noses and ears cut off, were sent to work on the First Emperor's roads, canals, walls, palaces or tomb buildings. Often their families were sent too. These harsh punishments made sure that everyone kept on obeying the Emperor.

There were rewards as well, for if the Emperor was always harsh his people might rebel. Officials who served him well were given houses and money. Loyal villages were sometimes given a couple of sheep once a year to roast for a feast. But there were more punishments than rewards.

The First Emperor set out to unite China. We know from archaeology that the states of China before 221 BC had different weights and measures, coins, farming tools, ways of using bronze, ways of burying their dead, different sizes of carts and different writing.

B SOURCE

The ancient records say the north gate of the Qin palace was made of lodestone (magnetic rock). It was said that the gate prevented assassinations because a visitor wearing armour or hiding weapons was immediately stuck fast to the gate.

From 'Ancient China's Inventions', by J.H. San, 1984.

A SOURCE

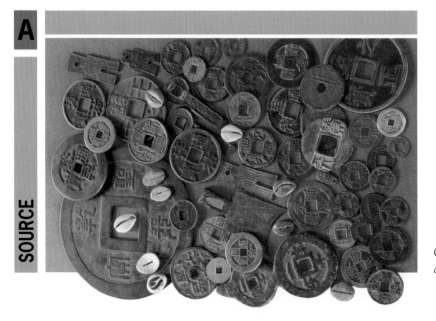

Coins and cowries from before and after the time of the First Emperor.

This measure holds about 0.2 litres. It dates from the Warring States period. The characters on the side are an edict (order) of the First Emperor's, saying that all weights and measures must be standardized.

The first thing the Emperor had to do was to make sure that all the Chinese people knew what he wanted them to do. His orders were sent out in writing. So he had to have the same writing all over China. Today, a person from the south of China cannot understand what a person from the north is saying, but they can both read the same newspaper. This is because the First Emperor made all the Chinese use one form of writing. Only 3,000 characters were allowed. This probably halved the number in general use before 221 BC.

Money is also very important in uniting a country. People are happy about buying things if they know they can take coins and spend them anywhere in the country. This encourages people to trade. Probably, the early Chinese people bartered – a pottery bowl for some meat, or a chicken for some rice. Later they may have used tools such as hoes and knives as a **means of exchange**. This would be something like three hoes for one goat or four knives for a sheep. Obviously full sized hoes were awkward to carry around. The answer was to make coins. The first coins were in the shape of the tools they had used as money before. Later, some places used cowrie shells. Cowrie shells made ideal coins. They were light, hard wearing, scarce, and impossible to forge. There were different coins all over China. The First Emperor swept them all away.

Instead, he had circular, bronze coins made. The coins were small with a square hole in the middle. After the coin was broken out of the mould it was threaded on to a stick for cleaning and polishing. The hole had another use. It made the coins light and they could be threaded on a string for safe carrying. These type of coins were used for the next 2,000 years.

Han Feizi

Han Feizi (280?–233 BC) was a member of the royal family of Han (see the map on page 10). He was a Legalist like Li Si. He said that in the past rulers could rule by being kind, but times had changed and harsh rule was now better.

The King of Qin (later the First Emperor) heard about what Han Feizi had said. He invited Han Feizi to work for him. Han Feizi said no. But later, when Qin was attacking the state of Han, he did go. When he got to Qin, he met Li Si. They had been students together, but Li Si did not want a clever competitor so he imprisoned Han Feizi and had him poisoned.

2.4 The Great Wall, Roads and Canals

The Chinese were afraid of the **nomads** who lived to the north of China. These nomads had no permanent home. They followed their cattle, sheep, goats and horses from one place to another, as they grazed. This was a very different life from the settled farming inside China. The nomads often raided the farms to steal wheat and other food. Over many years, the Chinese had built a number of long walls to keep out the nomads.

The First Emperor wanted to keep his empire safe. He also wanted to make sure that his black-haired people, as he called them, did not wander off to mix with the nomads. He ordered the building of a 'Great Wall' to join up and extend the walls already built in north China.

He sent many of his soldiers to work on the Wall. This helped to solve his problem of what to do with an enormous army in peacetime. However, working on the Wall was not popular. Many soldiers were **peasants**. After years of war, they wanted to go back to farm their land. Moreover, the Wall was in the cold north of China. It was built brick by brick, across mountains and deserts. The workers were made to build at a terrible pace and all the time they were being attacked by the nomads.

This part of the Great Wall of China has been rebuilt and restored. The actual distance of the Wall from west to east is about 1,875 miles (3,000 kilometres). However, there are lots of extensions and overlapping sections, adding up to about 3,750 miles (6,000 kilometres) of wall. Some historians think that, originally, it was longer.

A

SOURCE

Thousands of soldiers and convicts were sent to work on the Wall. Thousands of ordinary people were **conscripted** (forced) to build the Wall. So many died that Chinese historians called the Great Wall, 'the longest graveyard in the world'.

Watchtowers were built every few hundred metres along the Wall. The lookout soldiers kept in contact with each other by signalling. They used red and blue flags in the daytime and fires at night. The flag code was complicated. The soldiers sent detailed messages very quickly from watchtower to watchtower. All the messages had to be recorded. When they were received, they were written on strips of bamboo or wood. Many of these strips have been discovered near the Wall.

Road system

The bricks, tools, workers and even the food had to be brought to the Wall. A massive network of roads was built. They were part of the **imperial road system** started by the First Emperor. These roads radiated out from the capital city and were called 'fast roads'. They were made of packed earth and were very wide. They were so wide near the capital that the centre lane was reserved for just the Emperor and his messengers.

The First Emperor ordered that all carts, carriages and chariots had to have the same length of axle. It had to be 6 feet (about 2 metres). This meant that the wheels were the same distance apart so they only made one set of ruts in the road. This cut down on the wear and tear. No one knows why the Emperor chose the figure six. We do know that he became obsessed with magic and six was a magic number to him.

Like the Wall, the roads were built by convicts, soldiers and forced labour. The road that runs north from Chang'an to the Wall was built in 212 BC. The First Emperor put one of his best generals in charge of building it. This road can still be seen today, running beside a modern highway. Altogether the roads built by the First Emperor totalled 4,250 miles (6,800 kilometres). This is more than all the roads built in the Roman Empire some 400 years later.

Like everything else that the First Emperor did, his main aim in building the roads was to unite and strengthen his empire. He could then send his orders to all parts of the empire. Horses were kept at inns along the imperial roads. They were only for the use of the imperial messengers.

B **SOURCE**

The First Emperor ordered the building of roads, east to the uttermost boundaries of Qi and Yan, south to the extremities of Wu and Chu, around lakes and rivers, and along the coasts of seas. The highways were 50 feet (18 metres) wide and a tree was planted every 30 feet (10 metres) along them. The road was made very thick and firm at the edge and hammered down with metal rammers.

Written by a court official of the Han dynasty in about 178 BC.

Trade

The First Emperor also built roads to encourage trade. Rice, pottery and silk were loaded on to carts and traded between towns and cities. By 214 BC, the First Emperor had already made a lot of money by gathering a tax on goods being traded. He had a **tax surplus** (spare money from taxes) even after paying for his army and his building projects. The *Shiji* records that he could afford to send two sheep and some rice to every village in his enormous empire, as an end-of-year gift.

In order to encourage trade even more, the First Emperor ordered the building of canals. Two were started when he was still only the King of Qin. They were both in the original state of Qin. One of these has been constantly repaired and used for the last 2,000 years. The third canal was begun in 219 BC. It is only three miles long but it is built through the mountains to connect two tributaries of the Yangtze River. The purpose of this canal was to transport food and other supplies to the army stationed in the south of the new empire. It is still in use today.

C | One of the First Emperor's most famous reforms was to make all carts and carriages have wheels the same distance apart. This is always explained as being very sensible because the roads in north China are muddy and develop deep ruts. But this is a poor explanation. If all carts can travel in the same rut, sooner or later they will come to rest on their axles.

SOURCE

From 'The Treasures and Dynasties of China' by Bamber Gascoigne, 1973.

This map shows the roads built by the First Emperor. He also joined up and repaired walls which had been built earlier.

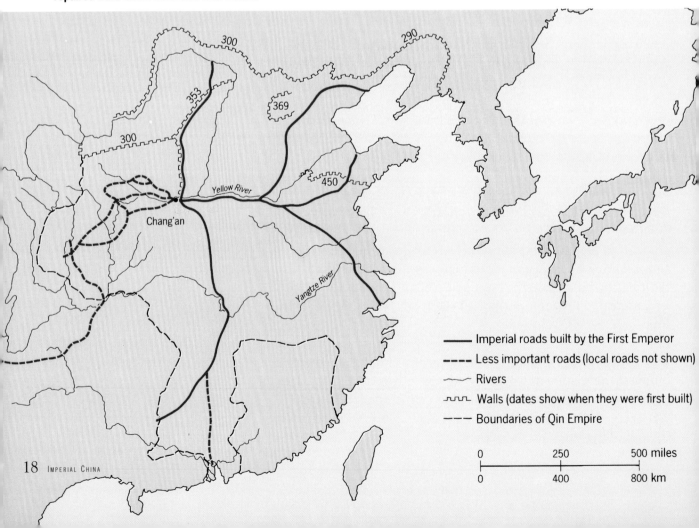

Imperial roads built by the First Emperor
---- Less important roads (local roads not shown)
〜 Rivers
ⅎⅎ Walls (dates show when they were first built)
--- Boundaries of Qin Empire

| 0 | 250 | 500 miles |
| 0 | 400 | 800 km |

Li Si

Li Si came from the state, or kingdom, of Chu during the Warring States period. It was a time of war but also of great learning. Li Si was one of many philosophers, statesmen and politicians who advised kings on how to rule their countries.

Li Si was also very ambitious. He saw that the King of Qin was going to conquer the other kingdoms. So in 247 BC he left Chu and journeyed to Qin. He introduced himself to the king, and soon joined the government. When the King of Qin became the First Emperor, Li Si was his chief minister from 221 to 206 BC. Li Si oversaw all the reforms and building programmes at this time. He was put to death by a later emperor.

Despite the Great Wall, the nomads were a constant threat. Pottery models of watchtowers, like this one, are often found in tombs of the Han dynasty.

2.5 Warfare – the Terracotta Army

Until the 1970s, we did not know much about the First Emperor's soldiers, weapons or ways of waging war. Then Chinese archaeologists discovered the **Terracotta Army**. They found over 6,000 life sized pottery soldiers guarding the tomb of the First Emperor. These soldiers were buried in huge pits.

Pit 1 contains over 3,000 soldiers, mostly **infantry men**. They are positioned in the corridors of the tomb. These foot soldiers are armed with bows, crossbows, swords, spears and dagger axes. They are in military formation, four abreast in nine rows, just as they would have been on the battlefield. The archers are in front. They wear no armour so they can fire their arrows and move quickly forward or out of the way. Most of the archers have crossbows.

Unarmoured foot soldiers stand behind the archers and then there are six **chariots**. There is one charioteer and one or two guards. The guards probably had 20 feet (6 metre) long bamboo lances to keep the enemy from chopping off the horses' heads. At least two of the chariots must have held officers who gave commands. They had drums and bells which could be heard all over the battlefield. It would make sense to have had the officers near the front where they could see what was going on.

A

SOURCE

Archaeologists digging out the Terracotta Army.

B

SOURCE

The Terracotta Army, standing in military formation.

C

SOURCE

Now gongs and drums, banners and flags make the soldiers pay attention. The brave cannot rush forward. The cowardly cannot run away. This is the art of employing an army. All do as they are commanded. When Chu fought Qin there was a keen officer who rushed forward and took a pair of heads before the battle started. He was praised as brave but the Chu general said: 'I am confident that he is an officer of ability, but he is disobedient.' Thereupon he beheaded him.

From 'The Art of War' by Sun Zi, written in about 490 BC.

The soldiers along each side of Pit 1 are wearing armour and facing outwards. The soldiers at the back are well armoured too. None of the soldiers wear helmets, but the officers wear caps of different sorts.

Pit 2 is smaller than Pit 1. It contains archers, chariots and cavalry. The First Emperor increased the number of horse soldiers. He dressed them in trousers and short tunics. They were faster moving than the chariots. None of the soldiers carry shields. They were not expected to stand and defend themselves. They always attacked. Thus speed was one of the most important assets of the First Emperor's army.

Pit 3 has 68 figures who might have been a special unit belonging to the Emperor.

D

SOURCE

The first impact was unforgettable. 5 metres (16 feet) below where we stood were the ranks of the Terracotta Army, a sea of faces, eyes staring ahead.

From 'The First Emperor of China' by Arthur Cotterell, 1981.

The Terracotta Army held real weapons. Robbers broke into the tomb not long after it was finished and stole some of these weapons, but not all. The wooden crossbows have rotted away leaving only the bronze triggers. Because of their power, crossbows were very popular. A shot fired from a crossbow was said to be able to penetrate any soldier's armour up to 200 metres away.

Most of the weapons are made of cast **bronze** which is an **alloy** of tin and copper. The bronze worker varied the quantities of metal in the alloy. Swords had a high tin content of 21 per cent. This made the hardness close to that of steel. Arrowheads had less tin, but had lead added. This made them cheaper to make. They were also very heavy so that they penetrated armour better.

Some of the swords in the tombs appear to have undergone some sort of anti-corrosion treatment to prevent rusting. After 2,000 years some are still shiny and can split a hair. Some of them even appear to have been treated with chromium for hardness and to stop them corroding. Methods of using chromium were not discovered in Europe until the 20th century.

The armies of the First Emperor were massive. Sometimes, according to the *Shiji*, he had as many as 600,000 soldiers. This is much larger than armies in later dynasties. The Han are said to have made do with anything between 130,000 and 300,000 men. The much later Tang dynasty is said to have sent some 150,000 soldiers against Korea. It is possible that the author of the *Shiji* is exaggerating. However, the First Emperor sent 100,000 men to build the Great Wall and 700,000 to build his amazing tomb. Considering the size of both the Wall and the tomb and how quickly these two were built, the numbers are not so surprising.

This archer is wearing light armour. Nobody knows whether his armour was made of iron pieces rivetted together or of specially hardened scales of leather. He wears a scarf to prevent the armour chafing his skin. The face of every pottery soldier is different. His bow has either completely rotted away or it might have been stolen by early grave robbers.

E

SOURCE

F

The armies of the First Emperor were not **professional** armies. He called up men when he needed them. At one time, any male over the age of fifteen could be called up to fight or work for the Emperor. Later dynasties did have professional armies. They paid their soldiers all the time. Professional armies usually have good soldiers but cost more to keep.

Many soldiers were stationed on the Wall. The large openings are for them to fire crossbows from.

'Soldiers'

'Soldiers' by an unknown poet of about the 1st century AD, translated by A. Waley.

They fought south of the ramparts,
They died north of the wall.
They died in the moors and were not buried.
Their flesh was the food of crows.
'Tell the crows we are not afraid;
We have died in the moors and cannot be buried.
Crows, how can our bodies escape you?'...

The riders fought and were slain;
Their horses wander neighing...
The harvest was never gathered.
How can we give you your offerings?
You served your Prince faithfully,
Though all in vain.
I think of you, faithful soldiers;
Your service shall not be forgotten.
For in the morning you went out to battle
And at night you did not return.

2.6 Irrigation

Li Bing was one of the First Emperor's **officials**. He was in charge of the district of Shu. This was an area near the River Min. The River Min is a tributary of the Yangtze River. Sometimes the river flowed sluggishly. It passed by fields dry from lack of rain. Sometimes it was swollen by rain-water from the mountains and flooded. The water poured over its banks and swept away whole villages.

Li Bing wanted two things. First, he wanted the river to run steadily. Second, he wanted the water in the River Min to be used to **irrigate** the fields around its banks. Bringing water from the big rivers was particularly important when growing rice. Control of flooding was important because Chinese rivers flood often and violently.

Li Bing organized thousands of peasants to work for him. They built an island in the river. On one side, the river flowed fast and deep on its way to the Yangtze. On the other side, it was made shallow and wide so it flowed more slowly. This shallow part of the river was channelled off into canals that led to irrigation ditches in the fields.

This type of water-wheel has been used for hundreds of years. It raises the water from the river, up to the fields above the river banks. The water is flowing from left to right in the photograph.

A

SOURCE

When the river was in flood, the water roared down past the island on both sides. If there was too much on the slow side, it would flood the fields and villages. To prevent this, a low wall was built to separate the two rivers at the east end of the island. It let the flood water over the top and back into the fast river. This irrigation system on the River Min has been repaired and updated over the centuries and is still in use today.

In 1974, a statue of Li Bing was discovered. It is made of stone and stands 2.9 metres high. Li Bing was very popular and more or less worshipped by local people. He had improved and even saved, many lives.

B

SOURCE

An official in a carriage. This bronze model was made during the Han dynasty, soon after the time of the First Emperor.

Po Chu-I

Po Chu-I (AD 772–846) was an official and a famous poet. Many scholars were officials and worked for the emperor as governors, inspectors or engineers. Some of them combined being artists or poets with their jobs of building canals, bridges or collecting taxes and governing remote parts of China.

Po Chu-I was born in AD 772. He worked for ten years at his studies and passed his examinations when he was 28 years old. He then had to wait for six years to get a job. After a period of being out of favour with the emperor, he was made Governor of the important city of Hangzhou. He was 40 years old. Three years later he was governor of another province but then had a year off work because he was ill. However, he recovered and worked for another six years before finally retiring due to illness. He had a stroke and was paralysed in 839 and died seven years later at the age of 74 years.

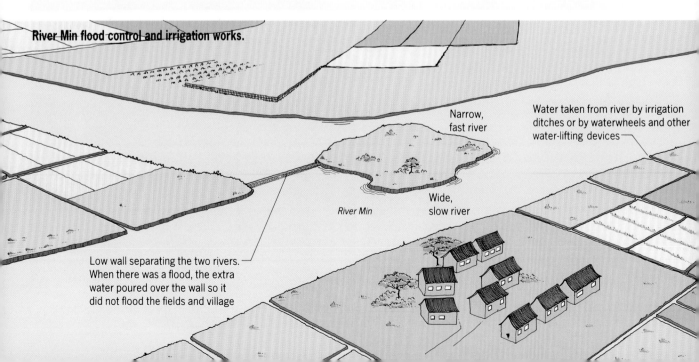

River Min flood control and irrigation works.

Narrow, fast river

Water taken from river by irrigation ditches or by waterwheels and other water-lifting devices

River Min

Wide, slow river

Low wall separating the two rivers. When there was a flood, the extra water poured over the wall so it did not flood the fields and village

2.7 The Death of the First Emperor

The First Emperor drove his people hard but they did not rebel. He pointed out that he had brought them peace and unity, trade and riches. As the years went by, the Emperor stopped appearing in public. This was partly due to his fear of assassination. He had many palaces built which were linked by covered roads. This was so that no one would know which palace he was in. Also he wanted to become godlike to his people.

He did not want anyone to look back to a better time in history so he gathered together all the books in China. Then he had them burnt. The only books he saved were books on medicine, farming and divination. This was because he thought they alone were useful. **The Burning of Books** was followed by burying over 400 scholars alive. It is pretty certain the Emperor burnt the books. No one is quite sure if he actually killed the scholars. His burning of history books so annoyed later historians that it is difficult to find any history book that has a good word to say for him.

The First Emperor wanted to be godlike. He wanted to live for ever. He paid **alchemists** and magicians to find him the **elixir of life**. He swallowed all sorts of potions of herbs and minerals (some of which may have been poisonous!) but died in 210 BC. The son who followed him was a weak man. He was as harsh as his father but far more greedy. By 206 BC, many people rebelled against him. The successful leader of the rebels was Liu Bang. He became the first emperor of a new dynasty – the Han dynasty.

A **SOURCE**

In the state of the enlightened ruler there are no books; obeying the law is the only instruction.

From the writing of Han Feizi in about 200 BC.

B **SOURCE**

The dynasty of the First Emperor fell because it failed to understand that the power to conquer and the power to hold what has been conquered are not the same.

Jia Yi, an historian writing in about 150 BC.

C **SOURCE**

A bronze monster mask and ring from the time of the First Emperor. This could only have been cast using the lost wax method.

Three stages of the lost wax method.

This diagram shows the lost wax method of bronze casting. When the bronze inside the clay mould was set and cold, the bronze worker broke the clay away to reveal the monster mask shown in Source C.

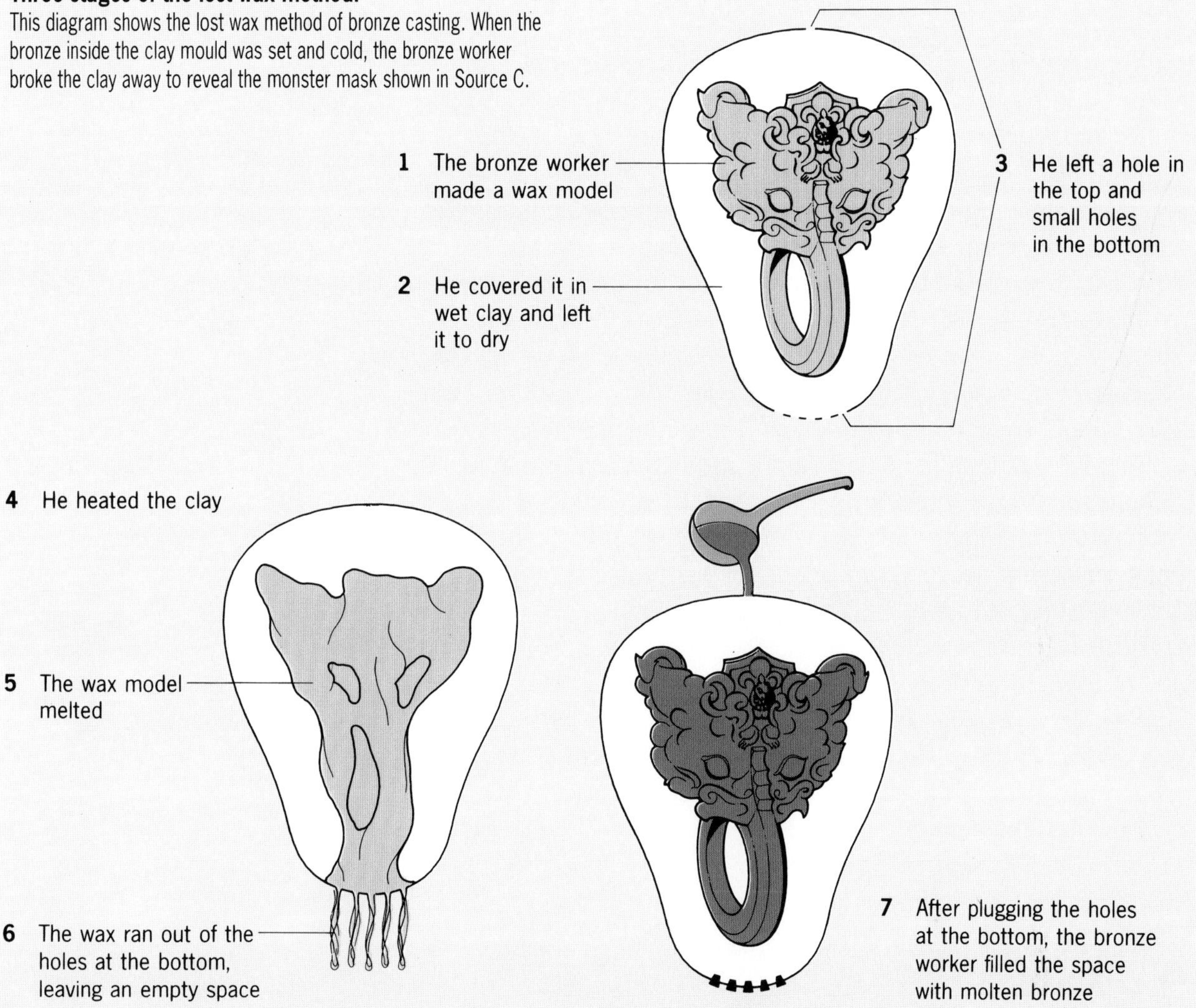

1 The bronze worker made a wax model

2 He covered it in wet clay and left it to dry

3 He left a hole in the top and small holes in the bottom

4 He heated the clay

5 The wax model melted

6 The wax ran out of the holes at the bottom, leaving an empty space

7 After plugging the holes at the bottom, the bronze worker filled the space with molten bronze

Mencius

Mencius (371–289 BC) lived during the Warring States period before the reign of the First Emperor. Mencius is the English form of Meng Tzu, meaning Master Meng. He is said to have been a pupil of the grandson of the much more famous Confucius. Generally he followed the teachings of Confucius and went around offering his advice to different lords of the time. Most of them liked him but ignored his advice. So, like Confucius, he decided to become a teacher. There is a book which was written about his teachings called *The Book of Mencius*.

Mencius taught two important things about ruling a country. First he said that rulers must be good; and second that all people should be good to their families. Rulers should think of their people as their families. Needless to say, none of these teachings appealed to the First Emperor. He much preferred to follow the harsher teaching of Li Si, his chief minister.

3.1 Confucianism and Ancestor Worship

Liu Bang was the first emperor of the **Han dynasty**. He was a peasant and probably could not read or write. But he was a good soldier and clever enough to listen to his advisers. These men were the officials and scholars. They made up the civil service which ran the empire (see pages 12–13). Liu Bang kept control of the empire in the same way that the First Emperor had. However, he rejected Legalism and excessive punishment, in favour of **Confucianism**. His rule was therefore less harsh. Confucius was the most important of all Chinese philosophers (thinkers). He lived in the 5th century BC. This was a long time before the Qin and Han dynasties. His parents died when he was young, but he managed to gain a good education and he became a wandering scholar. He wanted to advise kings on how to rule their kingdoms. He seems to have been rather difficult to get on with however. No king really wanted to give him a job, so he started to teach other scholars.

One of the main things Confucius taught was that older people knew better than younger people and the past was better than the present. (This was one reason why the First Emperor wanted to burn Confucius' books.) Confucius was very concerned with **good behaviour**. If people behaved well to each other, then all other problems disappeared. He laid down set rules of behaviour within families. Children obeyed their parents.

Part of the 'Sayings of the Court Instructress', a book which contained rigid rules about how to behave. It was made in the 4th century as a scroll, several metres long and 25cms wide. In this section the writing says: 'The beautiful wife who knew herself to be beautiful was soon hated. If by a mincing air you seek to please, wise men will keep away from you.' It is kept in a specially-built cupboard in the British Museum because it is in such a delicate state.

A

SOURCE

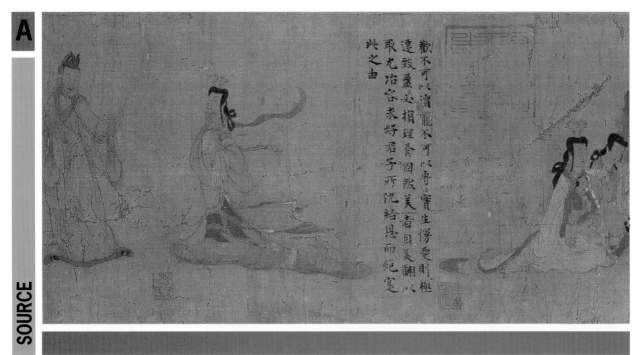

SOURCE

The tomb of the Emperor Chien Ling (AD 628 – 683) on the outskirts of Chang'an. There are more than 70 imperial tombs around Chang'an.

Wives obeyed their husbands and so on. There were rules for even the most distant cousins. If everything was clear and these rules were followed, no one would argue and fight. As the centuries went by his followers extended these ideas to the way kings and emperors ruled. The empire was like a large family and the emperor was the father. Of course, the father must not be too harsh. His behaviour must be good to his people too. This was where the First Emperor and his son had gone wrong. That is why the Chinese people had rebelled.

Liu Bang and the emperors of the Han dynasty followed the ideas of Confucius. In fact all future dynasties followed his ideas until the 20th century.

Confucianism was not a religion. It set out ways to behave on earth. The Chinese had long had religions that involved worshipping their **ancestors**. They believed in an afterlife, just like the life on earth, but where only spirits lived. These were the spirits of ancestors – grandmothers, great grandfathers, great-great uncles and so on. There were temples for worship and festivals to honour the dead of the family. Ancestor worship was why the Chinese were so keen to build huge tombs for important people with everything they would need in the next life. Ancestor worship with its respect for the family, fitted in well with Confucianism.

Confucius

Confucius or K'ung Fu Tzu (551–479 BC) was born in the state of Lu in the Warring States period. His father was a poor nobleman who died when Confucius was a baby. His mother brought him up until he married at the age of nineteen and became a government official. He became Prime Minister of Lu but resigned because he thought the ruler lived a wasteful and idle life.

Confucius began his travels. He went to other states teaching rulers and officials how to behave and run a civilized country. He was not interested in practical things like farming or trade. He wanted rulers to understand that they had responsibilities to the people they ruled, and that the people they ruled had responsibilities too.

3.2 Farming

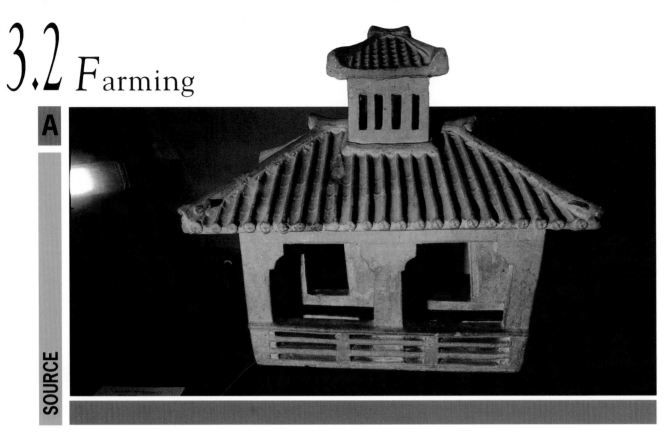

A *pottery model of a farmhouse from a Han tomb.*

Throughout Chinese history, farmers have been more important than merchants. The emperors recognized that the most important job was to feed all the people. Without food, an emperor had no soldiers, no officials, no craftsmen, no merchants and no empire.

Every spring the emperor went to **plough the first furrow**. This was made into a great ceremony. Everyone realized how important the emperor considered farming to be. Farmers were ranked after the officials in order of importance. This importance, however, did not make the peasant farmers rich. Although by the time of Han dynasty, most of them owned their own plots of land which they and their families worked on from dawn till dusk.

The valleys of the great rivers (the Yangtze River and the Yellow River) were fertile. In the north, the main crops were barley, wheat and millet for food and hemp for clothes. In the south, the main foodcrop was rice. Everywhere vegetables such as leeks, garlic, carrots and cabbages were grown as well as fruit. Iron ploughs pulled by oxen steadily replaced the old hand-pushed wooden ploughs. **Sickles** (for cutting wheat) and hoes were now made out of iron rather than bronze. This early use of iron which was much harder than bronze was far ahead of other parts of the world.

Everyone worked in the fields, although in some parts of China, the women took on the making of silk. The men did heavier work.

The farmer had many natural enemies. In the river valleys although the soil was fertile, the river could cause flood damage if it burst its banks. In other areas, there was not enough water to grow crops. The Chinese worked to bring water from the rivers by pipes and hand driven pumps. The population of China was large, so they needed to use every bit of land. They terraced the hillsides to make extra fields. They weeded and looked after every inch of their land by hand.

The emperors wanted farmers to learn about new ways of farming. Some officials wrote books about irrigation (see pages 24–25), rotating (alternating) the crops so that the land was not over-used and about new crops from other parts of the empire or beyond.

Whether they had good years or bad years, the farmers had to pay taxes to the emperor. This was to maintain the emperor, pay his officials, pay the army and pay for the gifts to the states on the edge of China to keep them friendly. When there were wars, the farmer had to leave his farm and join the army to fight. If there was no fighting, the farmer often had to spend time working on the emperor's building projects, like the Great Wall under the First Emperor.

Po Chu-I

From 'Watching the Reapers' by Po Chu-I, AD 806

A south wind blows
Suddenly the ridges
are covered with yellow corn.
The strong reapers toil...
Backs scorched by the sun...
Caring nothing for the heat,
Grudging the shortness
Of the long summer day.

An artist's reconstruction of a typical Chinese farm. The large building inside the walls was the granary. Very few large animals were kept because they ate too much. There was often a shortage of manure for the fields, so human manure was collected and used instead. There were always many people working on Chinese farms.

3.3 Trade and the Han Empire

Once Liu Bang was in control as emperor of the new dynasty, China conquered more and more land. The Han dynasty lasted about 400 years and was divided into two parts (with a brief rebellion in between). The first part (206 BC – AD 9), was called the **Earlier Han**. The second part (AD 25 – 220) was called the **Later Han**. During both periods more and more goods were traded in China with the outside world.

The great trade route between China, the rest of Asia and Europe was called the **Silk Road** (or Silk Route).

By 50 BC, the Han controlled the eastern end of the fabulous Silk Road within China. The Silk Road itself started in the city that the earlier Han emperors chose as their capital, called Chang'an. From Chang'an the Road went west. It ran westwards from China through mountains and deserts, with stopping places at oases. It passed out of China at a place called Dunhuang. It was the great link between China and the West, both Asia and Europe.

The Silk Road in the Earlier Han Empire.

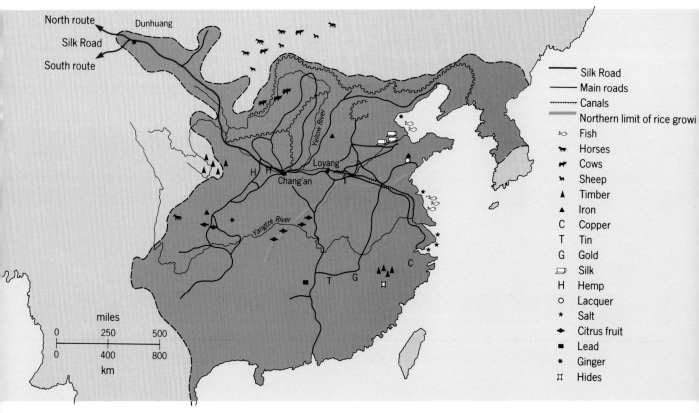

As well as carrying silk, the hundreds of camels that travelled the Silk Road carried spices, furs, bronze bowls, plates, weapons, mirrors and pottery from China. Probably the sort of goods that the merchants brought back from Europe and Asia were gold, silver, ivory and glassware, though nobody is quite sure.

Trade grew with the outside world as the empire grew. The Emperor Han Wu-ti even bought horses from the nomads of the north. They were bigger and faster than the Chinese ponies.

Trade within China grew too. The Han built more roads and more canals to make trading easier. Rice from the south was traded for sheep from the north. Salt from the east was loaded on to barges and shipped to the cities of the Yellow River. But, although trade grew and merchants became rich, they were still despised. Merchants were not allowed to wear silk clothes, ride horses or carry weapons. The great ambition of a merchant was to get his son to pass the civil service examinations and become an official.

Yet the great cities of China could not do without the merchants. Loyang became the capital of the Later Han Empire. Its population was about 200,000. This was made up of the emperor, his wives, his family and hundreds of servants. Then there were the officials who ran the empire. They lived in big houses with servants and office staff. Around them were gathered all the builders, carpenters, doctors, law officers and soldiers needed to keep the city going. They bought their food, clothes, silks, bronze bowls, jewellery, pottery and everything else from the merchants and traders in the markets.

The route of the Silk Road in the desert, running by a ruined granary that stored grain for feeding the soldiers guarding the western part of the Great Wall.

Liu Pei

Liu Pei (AD 160–223) was a member of the ruling family of the Han. He lived towards the end of the dynasty. The Han family had been ruling for nearly 400 years and, by the time that Liu Pei was grown up, there had been several weak emperors. This meant that local lords became more powerful and there was a great deal of fighting. To make matters worse there were droughts followed by epidemics of disease.

Liu Pei wanted to save the Han dynasty and restore peace and order. However, he failed to do so and died just after the fall of the dynasty. He is very well known to Chinese people because later on he was made a hero of stories and operas.

3.4 Industry

Traditional iron making shown in a 17th century drawing. Two men work the bellows to raise the temperature in the furnace in which the iron ore is melted. The molten iron then pours out of the furnace and into a pan to cool.

In the strong, large and fairly peaceful empire of the Han dynasty many industries, based on early Chinese discoveries and inventions, had a chance to develop. They included working metals like copper, bronze and iron, mining salt, making silk, pottery, lacquerware and paper (see pages 36–9).

Ironworking was the most important industry in Han China. Iron was used for farm tools and for weapons. The Chinese had already learnt how to make steel, blending irons that had different carbon contents. This steel was used for the finest swords. It was very hard.

Deep drilling for salt. Although this was drawn in the 17th century, the Chinese had been drilling for salt from the beginning of the Han dynasty.

Iron making was so important that the emperor made it a **monopoly** in 117 BC. This meant no one else could make iron. Only the emperor could own the 48 iron foundries. Each foundry employed between several hundred and several thousand workers. Often they were conscripts (ordinary people forced to work) or **convicts** (prisoners). But the Han emperors did not hold on to this monopoly. Within about a hundred years, other people had set up their own foundries.

Lacquer is the milky coloured sap from a tree called the Rhus Vernicifera (relative of the American poison ivy). When the sap is heated it turns black and looks like treacle. When it is left in a damp place it becomes so hard that it can be polished like glass. The Chinese used it to coat pottery and metal containers. They built up the lacquer layer by layer to make boxes, statues, shields and so on. Many lacquerware objects have been found in tombs. They last better in waterlogged tombs than in dry ones.

The method of making iron was supposed to be secret, like the making of silk. No one outside China was supposed to know how to do it. However, the knowledge filtered along the Silk Road. The Roman writer, Pliny the Elder (AD 23–79), wrote about Chinese ironmaking and how it had come to the West.

Salt making was another monopoly. Salt was used to flavour the bland millet and rice. It was also used to preserve food. At first, the Chinese took it from the sea. The water was boiled off and the salt was put into hemp sacks and sent to the cities.

However, the Chinese knew that great brine (salt) lakes existed deep under the earth. They could not drill down deep enough with their bamboo drills. But once iron was discovered there was no problem. They could drill to 600 metres, build a well, bring the brine up in bamboo buckets and put it, via bamboo pipes, into iron pans. The pans were heated over furnaces so the water boiled away. The Chinese tapped natural gas supplies from below ground. They burnt the gas to heat the iron pans. In this way they kept up salt production 24 hours a day.

Silk weaving was carried on in the emperor's workshops as well as by private farmers. Copper was mined and most of it used to make the bronze for coins. Only the emperor's workshops could make coins. Pottery was made all over China.

Needham

Joseph Needham (born 1900) is a British scientist who has taken a great interest in the scientific and technological history of China. He has researched and written about everything from mathematics and physics, to alchemy and acupuncture in Chinese history.

3.5 Inventions through Chinese History

The Chinese invented and discovered many things, sometimes hundreds of years before Europeans did.

Their scientific inventions include the **seismograph** to record earthquakes and the **hodometer** to measure distances in wheeled vehicles. Chinese **astronomers** were centuries ahead of the West too, in understanding the movements of the stars. This understanding led them to make an accurate calendar of 365 and a quarter days in a year.

They also invented some brilliantly simple everyday devices like the wheelbarrow. By using one wheel with a box on top, in the right place, a person could transport 100 kilograms in weight easily.

The dome of a tomb made in the 11th century BC. It shows stars and astrological details.

A

SOURCE

Another useful device was the breast harness for horses. Unlike the ox, a horse's shoulders are not suited to wearing a yoke as a harness for pulling. Anything round the horse's neck strangles the windpipe and not surprisingly, this cuts a horse's pulling power by about a half. The breast harness put all the weight of the cart lower down, on the breast bone. In the thousands of years before the steam locomotive and motor engine, horses, oxen, donkeys and camels were the most important extra power human beings had. Doubling a horse's pulling power was like doubling the power of an engine in a lorry, with no increase in fuel costs. The breast harness also worked for donkeys. Donkeys were brought from the West and were widely used. They were small, hardworking and cheaper than horses.

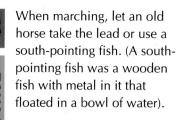

B

SOURCE

When marching, let an old horse take the lead or use a south-pointing fish. (A south-pointing fish was a wooden fish with metal in it that floated in a bowl of water).

From a military book by Zeng Gongliang and Ding Du, about 1044.

A hodometer measured the distance a wheeled vehicle travelled. The Chinese measured distance in 'li'. (One li = about 500 metres). Cogs changed the direction of movement of the wheels so that after one li, one figure struck a drum. Every ten li the other figure struck a bell.

Of all the inventions that the Chinese made, perhaps one of the most important is paper.

It is hard to imagine life without writing. Possibly ancient people piled up stones or tied knots in rope in order to keep a record of how many days had passed since the harvest or how many sacks of rice they had stored away.

Scratching, then writing on bones, shells, wood and bamboo followed. Archaeologists have found wood shavings near the Great Wall. The soldiers used them for writing practice. All of these writing materials are heavy and it is said that the First Emperor read and approved about 60 kilograms of documents every day! These documents were written on bamboo and strung together with leather thongs.

By the time of the Han dynasty, the search was on for something light in weight, long-lasting and cheap. Silk was light and long-lasting, but it wasn't cheap. The Chinese found that when second-rate silk cocoons were pulped to make silk floss, some stuck to the drying mat. When dry this could be peeled off in a sheet. It was smooth to write on. This was called **xidi**. But even with these second-rate silk cocoons it was expensive.

Arab merchants, commenting on fellow travellers in the 9th century AD.

Chariot and closed carriage found near the tomb of the First Emperor. Paper was used in hundreds of ways. Oiled paper was made into umbrellas and even raincoats.

D

SOURCE

The same process was tried with hemp. It worked and was much cheaper. The next step was further experiments, with other plants. Cai Lun was an official in the reign of Emperor He of the Han dynasty. He was an inspector of palace workshops. Cai Lun suggested that the papermakers tried using all sorts of things to make paper including bark, the roots of hemp, rags and old fish nets. The Chinese experimented with these or a mixture of them and from then on, papermaking flourished.

Cheap paper meant that people wrote more books. More books meant that more ideas were spread. They spread even more after printing was invented in the early centuries AD.

The pulped plant material was mixed with potash then steamed and mixed in a bath of clean water. The frames were dipped in and the pulp stuck to them. When dry, this pulp became paper.

Zhang Heng

Zhang Heng (2nd century BC) was a poet, a calligrapher (writer of very fine script) and a scientist as well. In about 130 BC, he invented a seismograph which he called an earthquake weathercock. It did not explain the reason for earthquakes, but it impressed the emperor very much because it told him there had been an earthquake, and also from which direction tremors had come.

Zhang Heng ran the emperor's observatory and made a number of discoveries. Among these is an improved armillary sphere which was better able to trace the paths of the planets in the night sky. He also invented some other astronomical instruments.

4.1 The Sui Dynasty and the Grand Canal

By AD 1, the population of China was 57 million. This was the first time a census had been taken. Han China had expanded in size and population. Despite a number of weak emperors and a rebellion in AD 9 which threw out the Han dynasty, the Han fought back and regained the imperial throne in AD 25. The Han ruled until AD 220 and were known as the Later Han. Since the capital Chang'an had been destroyed in the fighting, the Later Han moved to Luoyang. Trade flourished and Luoyang was soon as large and rich as Chang'an had been.

For three hundred years after the fall of the Han dynasty, China split into separate kingdoms. But between AD 589 and AD 618 the **Sui dynasty** united China once more. The first emperor of the Sui took the name of Wen Di. This means Cultured Emperor. He encouraged Buddhism in China. He was strong and like the First Emperor of the Qin dynasty, he wanted his dynasty to rule for a long time.

Wen Di's son was very ambitious. When he was emperor he decided to build new palaces for himself in both Chang'an and Loyang. He also decided to build a canal to join the Yangtze and Yellow Rivers. This was partly new and partly the joining up of existing canals and rivers.

There was a good reason for the new canal. Continual improvements to the growing of rice crops, particularly in new types of rice being grown, meant increasing yields. Therefore the hot, wet areas around the Yangtze River grew more and more rice. The population rose. Rice became the most important grain crop in China, followed by wheat and millet. The emperor wanted the rice from the south brought to his capital in the north. He needed it to feed his people. More importantly, farmers still paid most of their taxes to the emperor in grain, not in money. The emperor wanted his taxes to arrive safely in large barges at his capital.

A SOURCE

The Buddhist religion was encouraged. A 7th century Buddha from the grottoes at Yungang in north China.

B SOURCE

The written and archaeological evidence we have indicates that it was in the Sui dynasty (AD 589-618) that iron-chain suspension bridges first spanned 80 to 100 metre gaps across the great rivers of China. (Bamboo suspension bridges had been used before this time).

From 'The Legacy of China' by Joseph Needham, 1964.

C

SOURCE

The Grand Canal was the main north to south route until railways were built in the 19th and 20th centuries. It is still in use today.

The rice and other grains were stored in huge **granaries** owned by the emperor. The system was known as the **ever ready granary system**. In AD 605, there was said to be 50 years' supply of grain in case the harvests were bad. One harvest in every five was usually a bad one.

When the harvest was bad, the emperor gave grain free to the farmers. This prevented starvation and meant that the farmers had seed to sow for the next year. If the emperor did not do this, farmers (and therefore the whole basis of China's economy) suffered badly. This also helped the farmers from suffering at the hands of ruthless merchants. The merchants bought grain cheaply when there was a good harvest. They kept the grain until there was a bad harvest. Then they sold it to the desperate farmers at a high price. This sort of behaviour by the merchants was one of the reasons why the emperors and farmers did not like them.

The second emperor of the Sui forced hundreds of thousands to work on the palaces and the huge construction of the Grand Canal. He also set out to reconquer the area known as Korea. By AD 617, the Chinese people had had enough – they rebelled. The second Sui emperor was overthrown and a new dynasty was established.

Wen Di

Wen Di (ruled AD 589–604) was a soldier and made sure all the lordly families obeyed him. But he was kind to common people.

In 595, there was a famine. The emperor ordered his soldiers to help the poor people leave the city to find food. Wen Di felt that the famine was a sign of divine disapproval so he went on a pilgrimage, praying for forgiveness. Good harvests followed and people had plenty to eat. However, Wen Di was not so lucky. His wife plotted against his eldest son and so his second son became the heir. This second son was a ruthless man and killed his father.

4.2 The Tang Dynasty

Li Yuan, the first emperor of the **Tang dynasty**, had several clever, strong sons and grandsons. The dynasty, therefore, went from strength to strength.

The Chinese had believed for centuries in the **Mandate of Heaven**. They believed that emperors were not only wise, hard-working and brilliant soldiers but also represented the powers of the whole universe on earth. The emperor, they thought, ruled with the permission or the mandate of Heaven.

This was an important belief in Chinese history. The emperor was at the centre of a centralized state, like the spider at the centre of a web. Weak, careless, stupid or greedy emperors could not control the state and make sure the web was in good repair. When this happened, peasant farmers and warlords rebelled, nomads invaded from the north and the whole empire fell apart. The Chinese said that Heaven had withdrawn its mandate for that emperor to rule because he was not fit to do so.

The Mandate of Heaven gave the Chinese a right to rebel against a bad emperor. On the other hand, a powerful, successful emperor was widely supported because it was obvious that Heaven approved of his work on earth.

Heaven certainly seemed to smile on the Tang dynasty and trade flourished. They used the great city of Chang'an as their capital. It was the gateway to the West. Trains of hundreds of camels left Chang'an and skirted the 1,000 miles of Takla Makan desert, following the Silk Road, branching either north or south. They carried porcelains and silks. The merchants took with them Chinese ideas and inventions to the West.

Many of the merchants in China, using the Silk Road, were non-Chinese. During the Tang dynasty, the Chinese were more open to foreign ideas, religions (like Buddhism), food and goods than at any time before or until the 20th century.

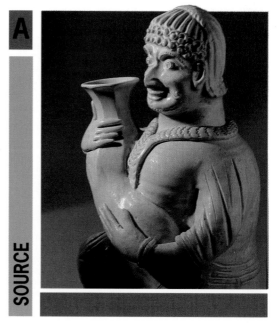

A SOURCE

A pottery figure of a foreign merchant. The Tang Chinese were both fascinated and repelled by foreigners. They thought them very ugly.

Li Shimin

Li Shimin (ruled AD 626–49) was the second son of the first emperor of the Tang dynasty. He did not spend a lot of money and he was very straightforward. The Chinese liked him and were pleased that they were united under a strong dynasty again.

He did not keep a huge army because it was too expensive. However, he did make sure that all the farmers had proper army training. Even when he became emperor, he insisted on drilling the part-time soldiers himself. He was particularly good at shooting the crossbow.

Li Shimin did not want a large army for another reason. A large army might have threatened his own power.

▲ A 7th century wall-painting on the inside of a tomb. The Tang aristocrats loved hunting and playing polo. They had copied these activities from other countries and from the nomads who were very good horsemen.

1 Imperial palaces   5 Main pleasure quarter
2 Imperial granary   6 Imperial observatory
3 Western market   7 Government offices of the officials
4 Eastern market

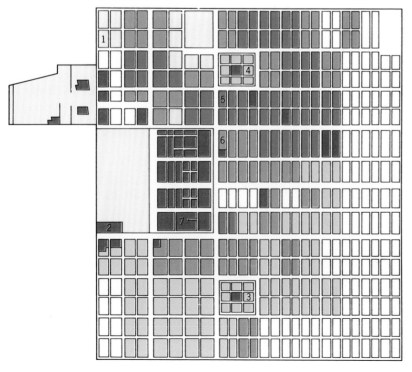

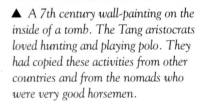

Residential districts:

Low class

Middle class

High class

Government buildings:

Palace

Market

Government offices

This plan shows Chang'an in the Tang dynasty. It was a huge city of one million people. The city was divided into walled wards (over 100) which were locked at night. There were over 100 temples including Buddhist and Daoist ones. There were over 100 merchant guilds. The markets have been partly excavated.

4.3 The Rise of the Song Dynasty

The Tang dynasty came to an end in AD 907. Rebellions against a weak emperor split China into five separate kingdoms called the **Five Dynasties**. In AD 960, an army general, **Zhao Quang Yin**, was proclaimed emperor by his soldiers. He knew there was a danger that other army generals would also try to become emperor. To try to avoid this, he called them to his palace. He gave them large pensions and kept them in the city where he could keep an eye on them. This stopped any more rebellions. Zhao became the first emperor of the **Song dynasty**.

The emperor's distrust of the army and the rise of the educated officials was good for Chinese government and artistic life. However, not having a strong army was dangerous for the empire. The nomadic tribes to the north were only just on the other side of the Great Wall. They could attack China at any time.

Wang Anshi was one of the greatest officials of the Song dynasty. Around AD 1050, he was living the quiet life of a provincial official, miles from the Song capital city, Kaifeng. At the time, the emperor was worried about the economy of his empire. He asked for suggestions. Wang Anshi sent in a list of ideas. The Emperor was so impressed by this list, he summoned Wang Anshi to Kaifeng and made him the chief minister.

The government officials divided into those who supported Wang Anshi and those who hated his new ideas. As long as the emperor was alive, he supported Wang Anshi, but when he died many of Wang Anshi's ideas were thrown out.

SOURCE A

Everyone knows that the army at the frontiers cannot be depended on to keep the peace. But since educated men think carrying weapons is a disgrace and cannot ride, shoot or understand how to fight a battle who is there left to fight but poor soldiers we have hired.

The debts of the government are due to spending too much, but also due to not looking for new ways to make money.

From the writings of Wang Anshi about AD 1050.

This is a list of some of Wang Anshi's ideas:

1 The emperor must make people pay higher taxes. The government was short of money to pay the army, maintain roads, give gifts to neighbouring states and so on.
2 The government must encourage farmers by giving them loans at very low interest rates. They could use the money to improve their farms and grow more food.
3 The government must encourage industry and trade. He suggested buying goods like pottery from the merchants at fixed prices. Then potters would know they could sell whatever they made. They would make lots of pottery and sell it. This would encourage trade. The more trade there was, the more money the merchants made, the more taxes they could pay to the emperor and so on.
4 The government should print paper money. It was easy to carry around. Backed by the government of the emperor, people would feel safe to use it and they would spend more money. This would encourage trade.
5 Waste land should be reclaimed. This meant more land for farming and therefore more land for taxing.
6 The government should have a good professional army. This would leave the farmers free to keep farming most of the time (and paying taxes to the emperor).
7 The peasant farmer should serve in the militia (reserve army) in case he might be needed to fight.

A market scene in early 12th century China.

Wang Anshi

Wang Anshi (AD 1021–86) passed his examinations at the age of 21 years. At first, he had a number of jobs far away from the capital city, Kaifeng. He was not keen to get involved in court life.

However, Wang Anshi was very clever. As well as being one of the emperor's officials, he was also a scholar who enjoyed learning, and a poet. He wrote more than 1400 poems. He had no interest in how he dressed or whether he washed. Many writers of the time pointed this out when they wrote about him when he was famous.

The emperor, at that time, was worried about the

Chinese economy. He insisted Wang Anshi should become the leading official. Reluctantly, Wang Anshi travelled to Kaifeng.

In 1069 Wang Anshi went ahead with all his reforms. However, many of them were very severe. Although Wang Anshi helped farmers by letting them have loans to buy seed at a reasonable rate of interest for the time (30%), the loans were compulsory. All farmers had to use this system and many did not like it. Wang Anshi also taxed all sorts of people like widows to raise money for the army. There was so much unrest that Wang Anshi resigned in 1076 and retired.

4.4 The Song Dynasty

During the Song dynasty, the Chinese were less outward looking than they had been during the Tang. One of the emperors did send ships out to explore. They sailed round to India and the Persian Gulf. This was before Europeans set out on their voyages of discovery. However, the emperors lost interest and no more ships set sail to the West. After all, the Chinese believed they were the centre of civilization and, on the whole, they found very little they wanted in the West.

The Song dynasty had growing problems at home. Wang Anshi had tried to shift some of the burden of taxes away from the peasant farmers. After his fall from power, his opponents (the high-up officials and rich people) made sure that the farmers paid all the taxes. Bowed down by taxes, the peasants rebelled in the early 12th century. Then in 1127, a northern tribe called the Chin, captured the capital city of Kaifeng. They took the emperor prisoner together with all his family. They were never seen again. Only one prince escaped.

People fled from the north in their thousands. **Li Chiang Chao** was one of China's most gifted women poets. She and her husband packed their bags, including collections of **porcelain** (fine china) and antique bronzes. They moved south. For three years, they kept moving house, further and further south. In the north, the Chin took more and more land. In 1129, Li Chiang Chao's husband was ordered to a dangerous province of China, near the fighting, to work as a local official. He decided his wife should stay somewhere safer.

A jar from the Song dynasty.

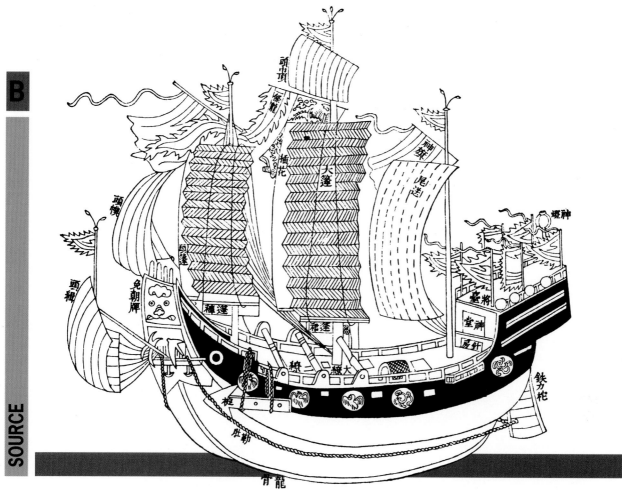

An 18th century drawing of a sea-going junk. The Chinese had lost control of the Silk Road. They turned to sea trading, particularly with Japan and the East Indies. They were already building large sea-going ships during the Song dynasty.

They parted and Li Chiang Chao did not see her husband again. He died of an illness. She wandered the country selling some of their valuable antiques to stay alive. In Hangzhou, she worked on her husband's book about ancient writings on bronzes and stones. When she published it, she wrote at the very end of the book about their life together.

After years of attacks by the Chin and fighting, the one prince who had escaped from imprisonment settled at Hangzhou. He became emperor of the Southern Song. The Song had lost half of China. However, Hangzhou was a lovely place to live and for the next hundred years, the richness of Chinese civilization continued there.

Hui Tsung

Sung Hui Tsung (AD 1082–1135) was the eighth emperor of the Song dynasty. He was a great patron of the arts, a famous painter and excellent calligrapher. Unfortunately he was not a strong ruler and found it difficult to deal with the northern tribes. The Song capital, Kaifeng, was captured in 1127 and Hui Tsung abdicated.

Sadly reclining on my pillow
Deep in the night I listen to the rain
Dripping on the leaves
Dripping on the leaves
That he cannot hear that sound again
Is breaking my heart.

From a poem by Li Chiang Chao, written after her husband's death.

5.1 Religion

A Chinese painting of Buddha found in the caves of Dunhuang and painted in AD 910. The writing in the green box reads: '...Offered in the hope that the Empire may be peaceful and that the Wheel of Law may continually turn therein. Secondly, on behalf of my elder sister and teacher, on behalf of the souls of my dead parents, that they may be born again in the Pure Land....'

In everyday life, most Chinese followed the ideas of Confucius (see pages 28–29). But this was not a religion. It was a **code of conduct** (a way to behave). For religion, the Chinese worshipped their ancestors or were interested in **Daoism**.

Lao Tzu lived at about the same time as Confucius. Lao Tzu's idea was that a person should follow the **Dao** or 'Way'. Daoists believed that a person should live in harmony with himself and with nature. They believed that after death people's spirits could live on for ever. Many people misunderstood the Dao. Like the First Emperor, they wanted to find a way to keep their bodies alive for ever as well. They looked for a special magic potion – the elixir of life.

Some Daoists set up temples and monasteries so that Daoism became a religion with gods and prayers and worship. Thus Daoism split into two: Daoists who followed the Way privately, living in harmony with themselves, those around them and with nature and Daoists who went to temples.

Into this mixture of religions and ways of living came **Buddhism** from India. It was introduced into China along the Silk Road during the Han dynasty. Many of the merchants on the Silk Road were foreigners to China. Many were probably Buddhists. They set up shrines to Buddha wherever they stopped along the Silk Road.

The Buddhists believed in **reincarnation**. When a person died he was born again. If he had lived a good life he was born higher up the scale. A good man might be reborn to become a Buddhist monk. At the very top a man became a **Buddha**. He was in harmony with the universe.

The Chinese welcomed Buddhism with enthusiasm. Like Daoists, Buddhists practised **meditation** (rather like quiet prayer for Christians). Normally people were absorbed in making money, working at their jobs, and living in their families. Buddhism and Daoism encouraged people to withdraw from everyday life at some time. This would be either for short periods during their lives or at the end of their lives.

Grottoes in Guangyuan. These grottoes were carved during the Tang dynasty and they have 7,000 Buddhas in 4,000 niches.

Lao Tzu

Tradition says that before Lao Tzu (604–? BC) was born, his mother admired a falling star in the sky one night. After this Lao Tzu was born as an old man of 62, with white hair, already speaking. He became an official in the capital city, Loyang, and had a son who was a soldier.

At the age of 160 years, Lao Tzu left Loyang in disgust at how everything was run. He travelled west and a gatekeeper asked him to write a book. This book is the famous *Dao Te Ching*. Lao Tzu continued on his way and was never seen again. He is said to be the founder of Daoism.

B

SOURCE

5.2 Silk

There is a legend about the discovery of silk. The Emperor Huang Di lived in about 2700 BC. He was worried because something was eating the leaves of his mulberry trees. His wife spotted some caterpillars and their cocoons. She found the cocoons were made of layers of soft fibres. As she pulled the fibres they broke. Later she discovered that if she boiled the cocoons the silk came off in long strands. She experimented using the strands to spin cloth.

Whether the legend is true or not, evidence has been found of silk from that time. Some oracle bones have Chinese characters for silk, mulberry and silkworm scratched on them. By 1000 BC there were silk workshops turning out clothes for rich people. They made banners, flags, curtains, screens and scarves too. By the time of the Han dynasty, silk making was the regular extra job of many women on farms. Officials even wrote books on how to raise and farm silkworms.

Court women preparing newly-woven silk from an early 12th century painting. This scroll is thought to have been painted by one of the Song emperors, Hui-zong.

B

Silk was produced in China at least 6-7,000 years ago. Neolithic stone ornaments in the shape of silkworms have been found in north-east China. Also archaeologists at a neolithic site in central China have dug up a silkworm cocoon cut in two. Further south, a bamboo box, 4,700 years old, was dug up. In it was a piece of woven silk.

From 'The Caves of a Thousand Buddhas' by R. Whitfield and A. Farrer, 1990.

In 1972, a Han dynasty tomb was discovered at Mawangdui (see also page 4). It contained many silk goods. There were heavy brocades and damasks, fine silk gauzes and embroidered silks. The colours ranged from crimson and dark brown to yellow, blue and white, with patterns of animals, flowers and clouds on them. Some of the silk was so fine that a simple shirt 128 cms long, with sleeves 190 cms long, weighed only 49 grams! Extremely long sleeves were popular among the rich, they were a sign that a person did not have to work.

The standard width for silk was 60 cms. A bolt, or roll, of silk was 12.2 metres long. In Han times, the price of one bolt of silk was the same price as 360 kgs of rice. Silk remained very expensive. In the Song dynasty, one scholar wrote to a friend apologising for sending ten rolls of a history book written on paper. He could not afford silk.

From the Han times long trains of camels carried the rolls of silk along the Silk Road. Each camel could carry 200 kilograms of weight. So the merchants could make good profits, despite the long journey to the West.

By the time of the Tang dynasty, the most important silk producing area was in the north. Different types of silk were being woven on more complicated looms. Later, in the Song dynasty, gold threads were woven into silk cloth too.

The Chinese kept the secret of making silk to themselves for many centuries. They exported it as a gift to keep neighbouring states friendly. They also sold it. But by about the 10th century AD, the secret had reached the West and other peoples of the world started making silk.

C

Gifts of silk by emperors during the Han dynasty

Date	Rolls of silk
51 BC	8,000
49 BC	8,000
33 BC	18,000
25 BC	20,000
1 BC	30,000

Throughout the Han dynasty, the emperors paid the wild nomads in the north to leave China alone. They usually paid in bolts or rolls of silk.

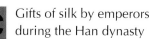

Huang Di

Huang Di (about 2697–2597 BC) means Yellow Emperor. He is a legendary figure. No one is quite sure whether he really existed. He is supposed to have been a great soldier who defeated all the warlike tribes around. He was given credit for inventing everything from magnetic compasses to coins for money (instead of shells). His wife was said to be very skilled in the running of a household and particularly skilled at making silk.

Many people look back to Huang Di as a very wise person and founder of China. He is supposed to have organized everything perfectly and then risen up into the sky to become immortal.

5.3 Clothes

Most of what we know about Chinese clothes comes from studying their tombs. This includes examining clothes buried in the tombs and paintings on the walls of the tombs.

Rich people wore silk. The emperor, the officials and important men of the courts wore one of two slightly different styles – the dragon robe or the court robe. These robes were both full length. They were made of thick satin for the winter and light silk gauze for the summer. The material might have a woven pattern in it or the pattern might be embroidered on to plain silk.

The women wore robes almost exactly the same as the men's. Both sexes wore all sorts of coats, waistcoats and embroidered collars over their robes for decoration or for keeping warm. The women usually wore trousers with tight cuffs at the ankle under their robes. Shoes were embroidered silk slippers or platform slippers on high wooden soles.

Of course the peasant farm people working in the fields did not wear long robes. Their short tunics and trousers were usually made of hemp, hemp woven with silk or cloth woven from a kind of nettle. Winter in north China was bitterly cold so the clothes were made of two layers of cloth with padding in between.

The Chinese were very keen to keep everyone in their right place in society. This followed from their belief in Confucianism. Confucius had said that the best way to run a home or an empire was to be orderly and everyone to know her or his place. The robes of the court officials, the army commanders and the emperor's concubines reflected this belief.

The Chinese had **dye workshops** as early as 3000 BC. They used vegetable dyes to make colours of blue, yellow, red, white and black, to dye their clothes. There were rules about who could wear special colours.

A silk robe found in the Han tomb at Mawangdui.

Only the emperor could wear yellow and have a special five-clawed dragon embroidered on his robes. An official of the first rank could wear an embroidered crane, the second rank, a golden pheasant, the third rank a peacock and so on down to the ninth rank. The army had the same system. The first rank wore a unicorn, the second a lion, down to the ninth who wore a rhinoceros.

Court ladies from the Tang dynasty, from a wall-painting in a tomb.

A Girl's Life

From a poem where a mother-in-law sends her son's wife back to her own home.

'Child,' cries her mother,
and loud she claps her hands,
'We little thought to see you
 home so soon.
For at thirteen I taught you to
 weave silk,
At fourteen you could cut clothes.
At fifteen you played the lute.
At sixteen you knew customs.
At seventeen I sent you to be
 a bride.'

5.4 The Empress Wu and Examinations

When the second Tang emperor died, his lower rank concubines shaved their heads and entered Buddhist monasteries. The new emperor, Gao Zong, however, fell in love with one of the concubines. Her name was **Wu Zhao**. He brought her out of the monastery. Within a couple of years, he had abandoned his childless wife and made Wu Zhao the empress. She immediately had the wife and one of the emperor's favourite, high-ranking concubines murdered. Their arms and legs were cut off and they were left to die in a wine vat. After this Wu Zhao had almost complete control of the emperor. So much so, that by the time he died in AD 683, she really ran the empire.

Two weak emperors reigned for a few years, but in AD 690 the second one was thrown out by Wu Zhao and she declared herself empress. This was the first and only time the Mandate of Heaven was given to a woman. Many of the rich, aristocratic families did not like her and feared her power. She placed her trust in the officials who had passed their **examinations**. They owed their jobs to her and so they supported her.

For a long time, young men had sat examinations in order to become officials in the civil service. But often, rich people had been able to become officials without passing these exams.

A

SOURCE

A tomb guardian from the Tang dynasty. Tomb guardians were very popular in Tang times, one was often placed at each corner of a tomb to keep away evil spirits. The Empress Wu had a magnificent tomb built for her, with the road to it lined with stone tomb guardians.

B

SOURCE

That year, there was a special examination. The young man took the paper in criticism of the government and advice to the emperor. He came out top and was appointed Army Inspector at Chengdu. Now he was an official.

From 'Story of a Singsong Girl' by Bai Xingjian, written during the Tang dynasty.

C

SOURCE

In the Royal City spring is almost over,
Tinkle, tinkle – the coaches and horsemen pass
We tell each other. 'This is the peony season';
And follow with the crowd that goes to the Flower Market...
There happened to be an old farm labourer
Who came by chance that way.
He bowed his head and sighed a deep sigh;
But this sigh nobody understood.
He was thinking 'A cluster of deep red flowers
Would pay the taxes of ten poor houses'.

A poem by Bai Juyi, written about AD 810. He was a high official. For some time he was in charge of engineering works at a lake at Hangzhou.

These people were aristocrats whose families had been rich and important for a long time. Under Empress Wu, the examinations became the most important way of choosing officials. Boys from the country had to be recommended by the local official. Young men from all over China had the chance to sit examinations and if they passed, to replace the aristocracy in official positions. The fact that it took years of study and only about ten per cent passed did not stop thousands of men from trying.

They sat the examinations in separate cubicles (small rooms). The doors to the cubicles were locked. The young man was on his own to answer the questions. (In the time of the Han dynasty each man had to fire an arrow at the examination question paper. He had to answer the question he hit. The Chinese were very keen to stop cheating.)

There were different levels of examinations for district, provincial and central officials. Some of the examinations were in special subjects such as law and mathematics. These were not the most important. What the empress (and the emperors) were looking for were top executives to run the empire. The examiners were looking for men who were well educated in Confucianism. They also had to be able to write well and show outstanding judgement in the sort of decisions that were needed when running a huge empire. The examination system under Empress Wu produced very well educated and cultured men.

Although there was no formal education for women, there is enough evidence of cultured women for it to be obvious that there was a tradition of learning in the homes of the families of officials and aristocrats.

Li Po

Li Po (AD 701–62) is probably one of China's most famous poets both inside and outside China. There is a famous book of the Tang dynasty called *Three Hundred Poems of the Tang Dynasty*. Twenty-six of the poems are by Li Po.

He spent most of his life wandering, though he did spend a short time in the capital, Chang'an (Xian). He did a little work for the emperor because he was very clever, but he drank too much so he was never given very important work to do. He was so well known as a drunkard that many drinking houses were called The House of Li Po.

He, himself, said that he was a 'banished immortal'. This was a Daoist belief that any immortal who misbehaved in heaven was sent back to earth. He had to live out one life on earth as a punishment before he could go back to heaven. Banished immortals were always unusual and eccentric people.

5.5 Gunpowder

The Chinese made **gunpowder** from charcoal, saltpetre and sulphur. They were already using sulphur and saltpetre to cure skin diseases during the Han dynasty and they knew how to make charcoal. But it was not until the Tang dynasty (AD 618–907) that Sun Simiao wrote the **Book of Medicinal Powder** in which he gave a recipe for gunpowder. It did not stay as a medicine for long. By AD 919 it was used as the fuse for all sorts of fire weapons.

The earliest weapons were the **fire arrows**. A ball of gunpowder was wrapped around the arrowhead, the fuse was lit and the arrow fired. Then came **fire artillery**. This was when a fuse was lit on a ball of gunpowder which was then catapulted towards the enemy, flaming fiercely.

In the Song dynasty, the statesman Wang Anshi encouraged the development of gunpowder weapons and set up an **arsenal** to make gunpowder weapons at Kaifeng. He was particularly worried about the tribes of nomads who threatened China from the north. At a battle in AD 1083, 250,000 fire arrows were used. The Chinese won.

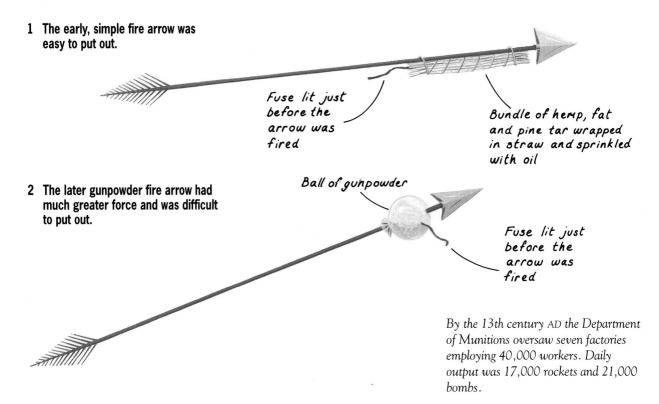

1 The early, simple fire arrow was easy to put out.

Fuse lit just before the arrow was fired

Bundle of hemp, fat and pine tar wrapped in straw and sprinkled with oil

2 The later gunpowder fire arrow had much greater force and was difficult to put out.

Ball of gunpowder

Fuse lit just before the arrow was fired

By the 13th century AD the Department of Munitions oversaw seven factories employing 40,000 workers. Daily output was 17,000 rockets and 21,000 bombs.

The next important development in the use of gunpowder weapons was the invention of a tube-shaped weapon. The first of these **fire guns** was invented in AD 1132 by Chen Gui. He filled a long bamboo pole with gunpowder. This was set alight and used to burn the enemy. Then came **firing bullets**. A bamboo tube was filled with gunpowder and pellets. When the gunpowder was lit the pellets shot out with a bang. This was probably the first gunfire the world had ever heard. By the 14th century, the Chinese were making the barrels of their guns out of metal. They were also hurling large hand grenades.

A fire dragon was a two-stage rocket. It was a one-and-a-half metre long tube made to look like a dragon. It was not perfected until after the Song dynasty.

Sun Tzu

Sun Tzu (about 4th century BC) is supposed to have written a book called *The Art of War*. However, parts of the book must have been added by a later author.

Sun Tzu's biography was written in the dynastic histories 200–300 years after his death. He taught kings how win battles and wars. His book was used for hundreds of years. It was even translated into French in 1782 and admired by Napoleon.

5.6 Medicine

The Chinese looked after their health very carefully. Chinese doctors used thousands of different plants as medicines. They also used **acupuncture**.

It is most likely that acupuncture was discovered by chance. A person in pain pressed a part of his body and the pain went away. Gradually, it was found that if you pressed different points on the body it helped to heal different illnesses. The Chinese then found it was even better to use fine needles to touch the points below the skin.

Sometimes, they used a herb called *Artemisia Vulgaris*. It was rubbed in the hands into a cone shape, placed on an acupuncture point and lit. The effect was to spread warmth into the body and therefore healing. This was called **moxibustion.**

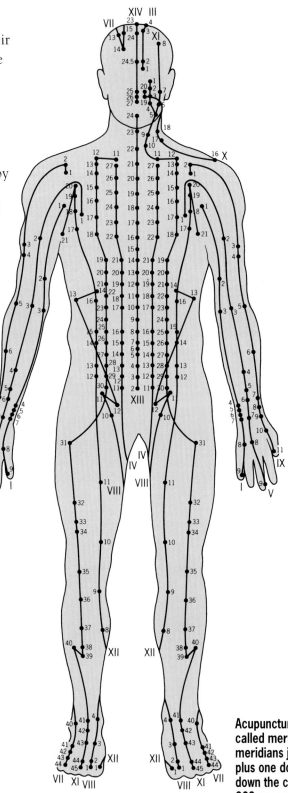

Acupuncture points are joined in groups called meridians. There are twelve main meridians joining acupuncture points, plus one down the centre front and one down the centre back. There are about 360 acupuncture points in general use.

Obviously it was important to know which acupuncture points to use to make people well again. Doctors trained for years to learn all the herbs and their uses and to know all the acupuncture points.

The Chinese said that as well as a blood-supply running around our bodies, there is also an energy-supply. This is the **Qi** or life energy. It runs along lines or **meridians**. Each meridian is connected to an organ of the body. When we are well, the energy flows freely along the meridians. We do not become ill. If however, the meridians are blocked in some way, the system does not run smoothly. We become ill.

The Chinese were very interested in **preventative medicine**. One tradition in China was that you paid your doctor all the time you were well. But, you stopped paying him when you became ill. He had failed. At some periods in Chinese history, you not only stopped paying him, but he had to keep you and your family until you were well again.

It was believed that the best way to live a healthy life was to visit your doctor about four times a year for a check-up. He examined you and then gave a treatment with needles, moxibustion or herbs, to keep your energy flowing freely. If you lived a sensible life-style (taking exercise, not eating or drinking too much, not overworking etc.) you should not become ill.

Of course, people did become ill. Either they were not born very strong or things happened that made them ill. Then they visited a doctor for herbal medicine and acupuncture. This got their system to work as well as it possibly could.

Huan

The prince of the state of Qin was seriously ill and had a dream of two young men who were inside him discussing his disease. One said, 'Huan is a clever doctor; he will do us great harm.' The other said, 'Let us hide between the heart and diaphragm. No one can reach us there.'

Doctor Huan (about 580 BC) arrived and examined the prince. 'This disease is incurable,' he said. 'It has settled in the region between the heart and the diaphragm. No needle can penetrate. No drug can reach it.' The prince exclaimed, 'What an excellent doctor!'

A SOURCE

Running water is never stale and a door hinge never gets wormeaten.

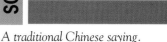

A *traditional Chinese saying.*

B SOURCE

When I visited China a few years ago, I witnessed a woman, fully conscious, having a thyroid operation – with just four needles blocking the pain.

J.H. Moore writing to the author in 1990.

C SOURCE

In a Japanese prisoner of war camp during the Second World War, the British soldiers were suffering from malnutrition, low morale and illnesses of all sorts. A group of Chinese prisoners were brought in. They set to work sharpening up little wooden sticks and doing acupuncture. In a short space of time they had cured the scurvy in the camp, yet there had been no increase in the supplies of Vitamin C.

Recounted to the author.

5.7 Life in the Song Dynasty

The Diamond Sutra is the world's earliest printed book that has survived. It is printed from six blocks and dated AD 868. It was found in the Buddhist Caves in Dunhuang by a British archaeologist in the early part of the 20th century.

By the time of the Song dynasty, life in China had changed in two main ways. Improvements in farming (particularly the discovery of new kinds of rice that yielded bigger crops) meant that the south of China became more populated and more important than the north. At the same time the nomads to the north of China became stronger and more threatening. As a result of both these things, the Chinese settled in a smaller empire, based around the rich basin of the Yangtze River.

A model of the Chinese Water Clock built in the Song Dynasty. Read Source C for a descripion of how this would have worked.

The capital of the Southern Song was at Hangzhou and, for the rich, there were often days of picnics and pleasure outings in barges on the beautiful lakes. The markets in Hangzhou were full of exotic goods from the West, foreigners and stalls of fresh fruit and vegetables from the countryside around.

When the Song lost the north half of China, they also lost control of the Silk Road. Because of the loss of this trading route, the Song became much more interested in building up a navy and trading by sea. That was how many of the goods reached China in the Song dynasty. They also took less interest in the outside world than they had done in the Tang dynasty. Perhaps this was because there were fewer foreign merchants in China and they were more cut off.

Life for the officials went on much as usual. Having passed their years of study, they lived well. They worked hard until they retired. Then they had a pension which was often half of the salary they had earned.

During his working life, an official might have breaks in his work too. Mothers and fathers were extremely important in Chinese life. When a parent died, the children went into **mourning** for three years. As well as grieving, the official had to stop work for this time. It gave him a break from working as a Confucian government official. At last he could follow the Dao in quietness. Su Dongpo spent his time in mourning ploughing his ten acres of land and nagging local officials to sort out cases of injustice to local people. In the evenings, he entertained his friends with wine. They discussed painting and poetry. Sometimes they wrote poems during the evening in their beautiful **calligraphy** (handwriting). Sometimes they played chess.

One invention that blossomed during the Song dynasty was **printing**. The Chinese had already invented paper. By inking paper and pressing it on words carved in stone, they invented printing. Printing meant books. Books meant the spread of ideas. In the course of many centuries, ideas on war, religion, making things, inventions and discoveries have changed the world. By the time of the Song, there were plenty of books so that more men could study to become officials, doctors and so on.

From information in the Science Museum, London, describing the working of the model clock built in the 1960s.

Ghengis Khan

Ghengis Khan (1167–1227) means 'Emperor within the Seas'. His father was a Mongol chief who died while Ghengis was young. Through his skill as a leader and fighter he rose to be king of all the Mongol tribes by 1206.

He next turned his attention to China and invaded from the north. During his lifetime he held the largest empire of land the world has ever seen, hence his title Emperor within the Seas.

5.8 The Mongol Invasions

China was fertile, rich and civilized. To the west and south lay mountains and jungles. To the north lay the cold lands on the other side of the Great Wall. There, the nomads lived in tents, following their herds of sheep and goats. Down the centuries waves of nomads had invaded China. They were either beaten back or they settled down and in a short space of time became Chinese. This was because they did not really want to destroy China. They just wanted a share in the people's riches and settled, comfortable way of life.

The Chinese were always aware of the danger from nomadic tribes. Since the Han dynasty, they had paid the peoples on their borders to be friendly. They usually paid them with silk. (At one time there was so much silk in the border countries that no one wanted it any more). The Han emperors also gave the leaders of tribes titles and official **seals** for stamping documents. Then they felt they were a part of the great empire.

B SOURCE

We cannot hope to recapture the terror that the mounted horsemen struck when they first appeared. For the rider is more than a man; he is head high above the other and he moves with bewildering power and speed.

From 'The Ascent of Man' by J. Bronowski, 1973.

A painting showing Mongol horsemen. From an Arab history of the world written in the 13th century.

A SOURCE

Another way the emperors tried to keep peace was to take **hostages**. Sons of the tribes' rulers were sent to the Chinese capital. As long as their tribe was friendly they were kept in luxury and educated. Another bribe was to send Chinese princesses as brides for the tribes' rulers. One advantage of this was that the princesses took Chinese ideas and ways of living to the border countries. Another advantage was that the children of the marriage were half Chinese and therefore were more friendly towards China in the long run. These methods, combined with a strong army, worked fairly well, although they cost the Chinese a great deal. However, by the 13th century the northern nomads had become more aggressive and restless than they had ever been before.

Led by **Ghengis Khan**, the **Mongol hordes** swept south into China and west across Asia into Europe. They conquered more land than any armies have ever done, before or since. Yet once they had taken China, they had nothing of their own to offer. So they settled down to become Chinese and to run China in the way the Chinese had. By the time **Kublai Khan** (Ghengis Khan's grandson) was ruler, he was calling himself Emperor of China and living in luxury, surrounded by his officials, wives and court.

Polo

Marco Polo (AD 1254–1324) travelled to China with his uncle when he was very young. He returned when he was grown up and became a favourite of the emperor Kublai Khan, the grandson of Ghengis Khan. He became an official and worked for the emperor for many years. He left China in about 1290.

Back in Europe he was taken prisoner in a war. A fellow prisoner wrote down the tales that Marco told.

Pottery models of actors and dancers from the time of the Mongol emperors. The Mongol conquerors enjoyed the same pleasures and pastimes as the Chinese – hunting, watching acrobatics, drama, art, poetry and dancing.

C

SOURCE